Karin Offender



*Have a question or concern? Let us know.*

*www.goodstore.me | info@goodstore.me | karinoffender@gmail.com*

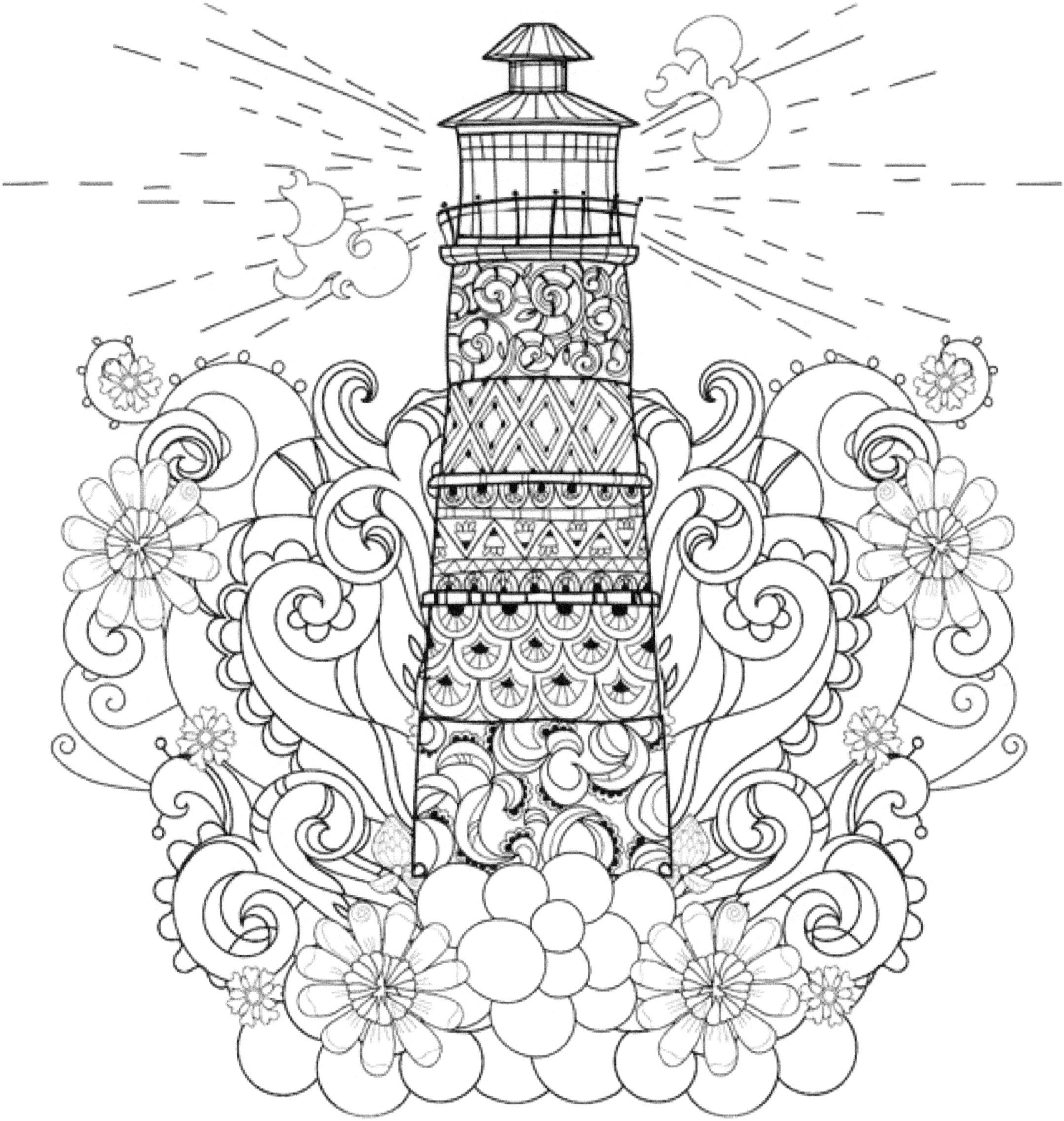

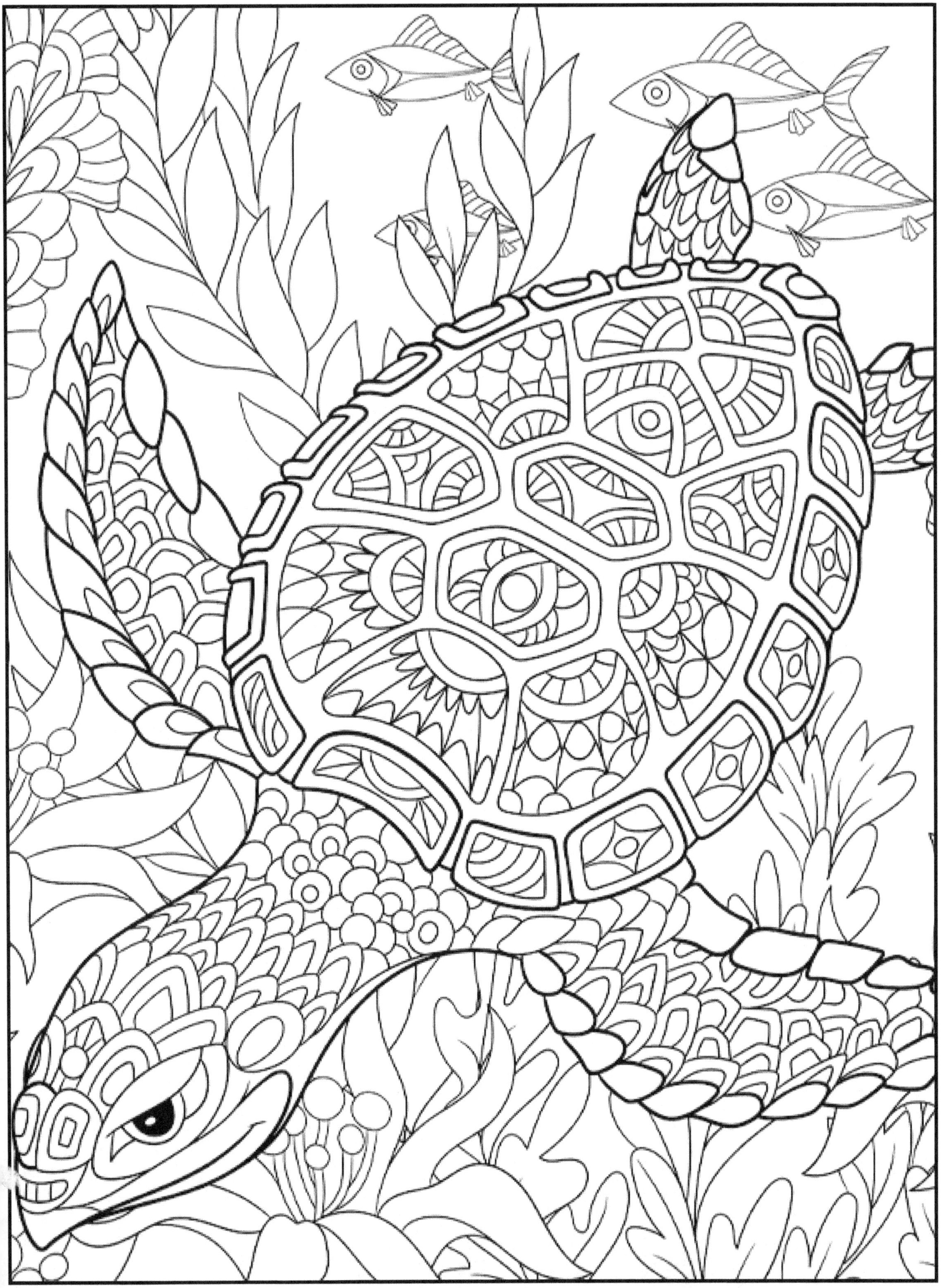

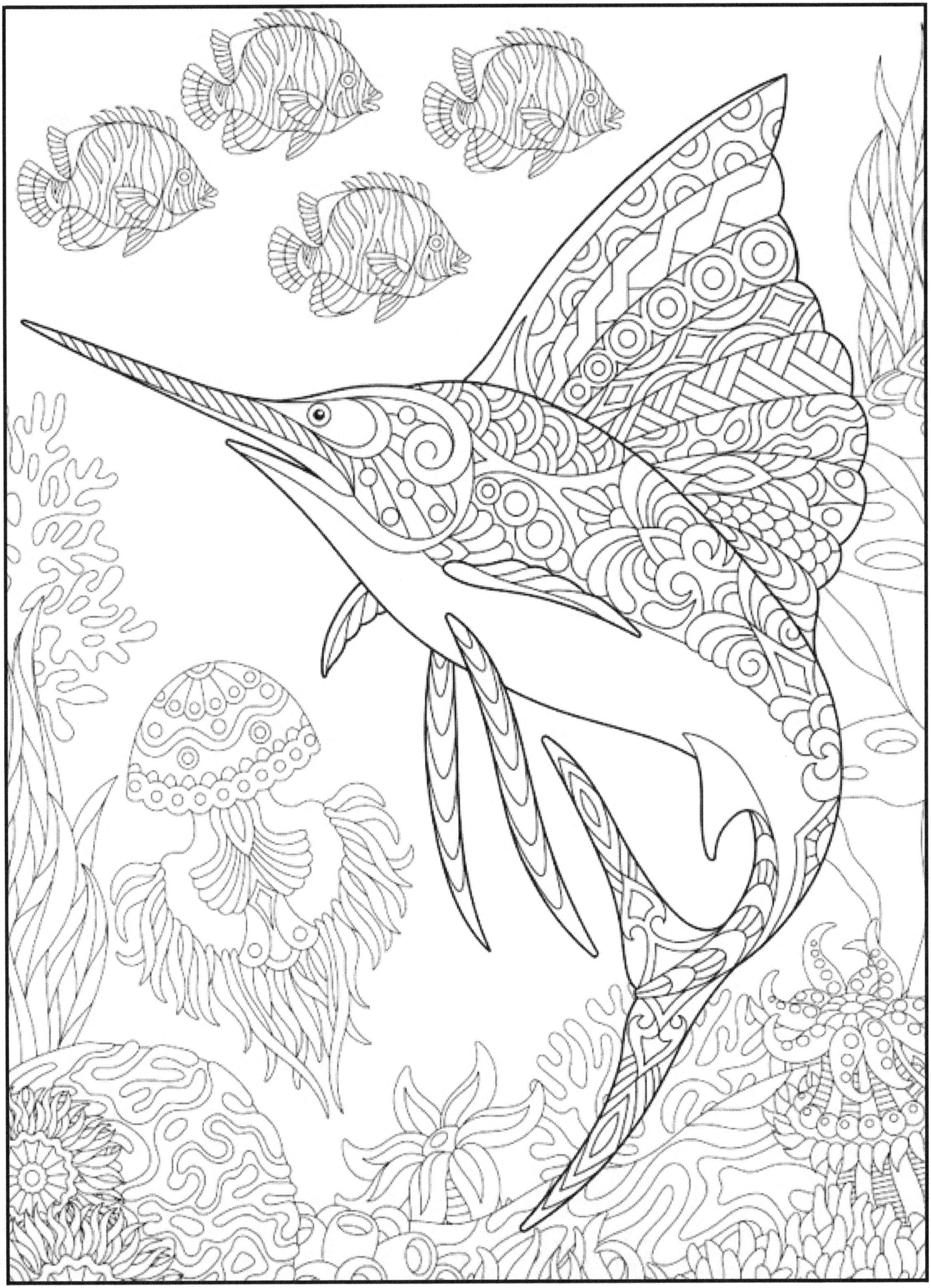

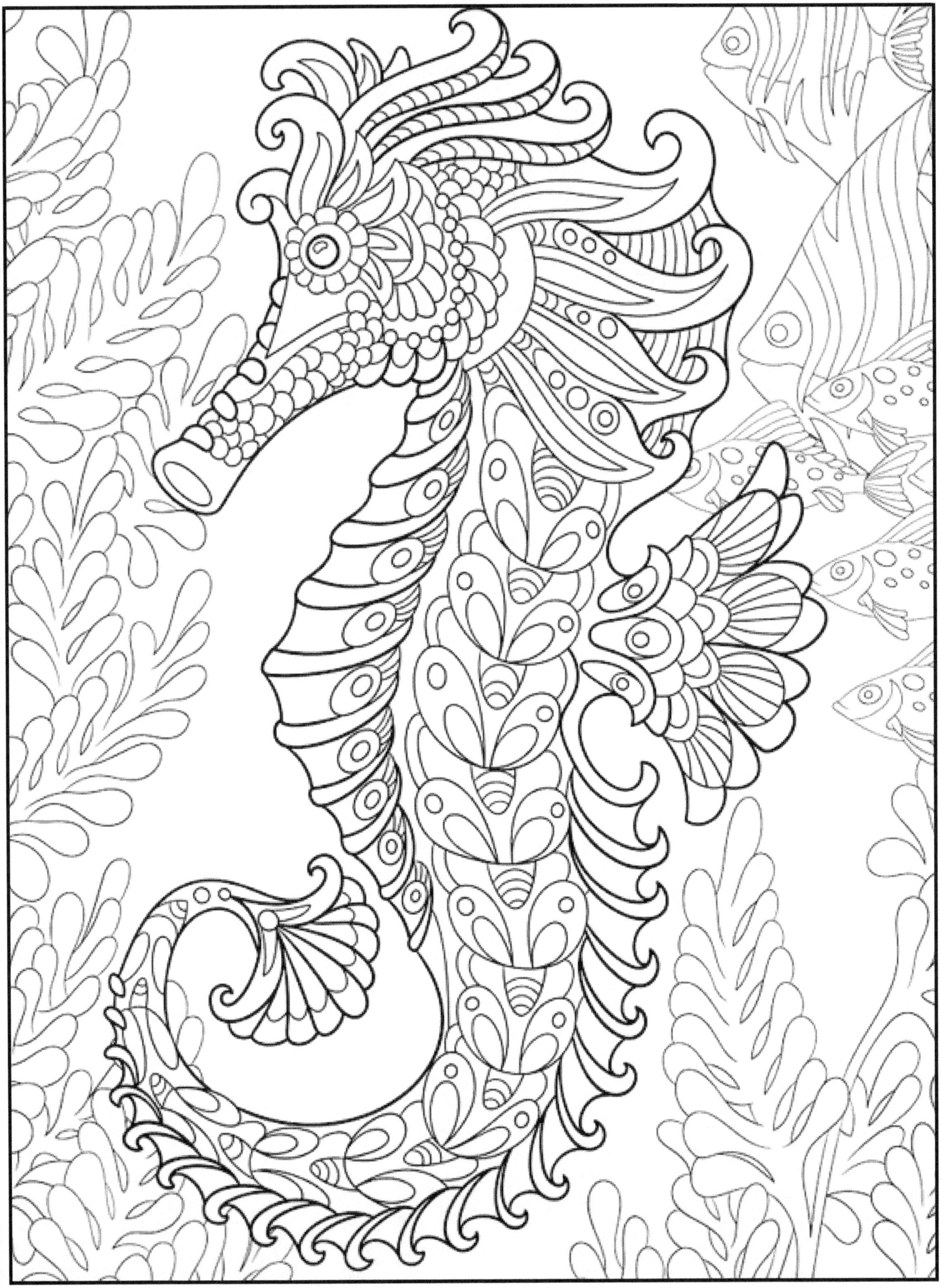

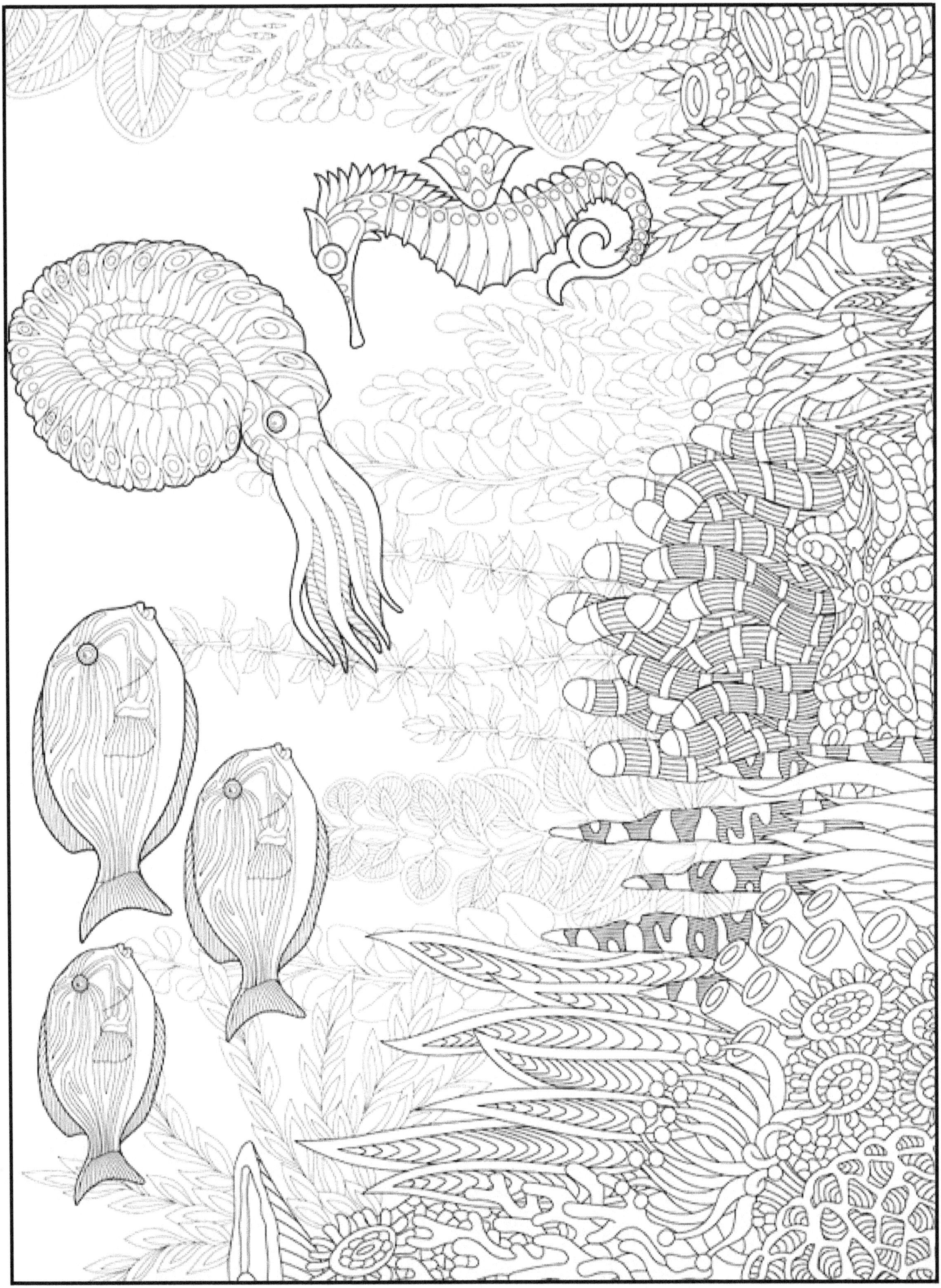

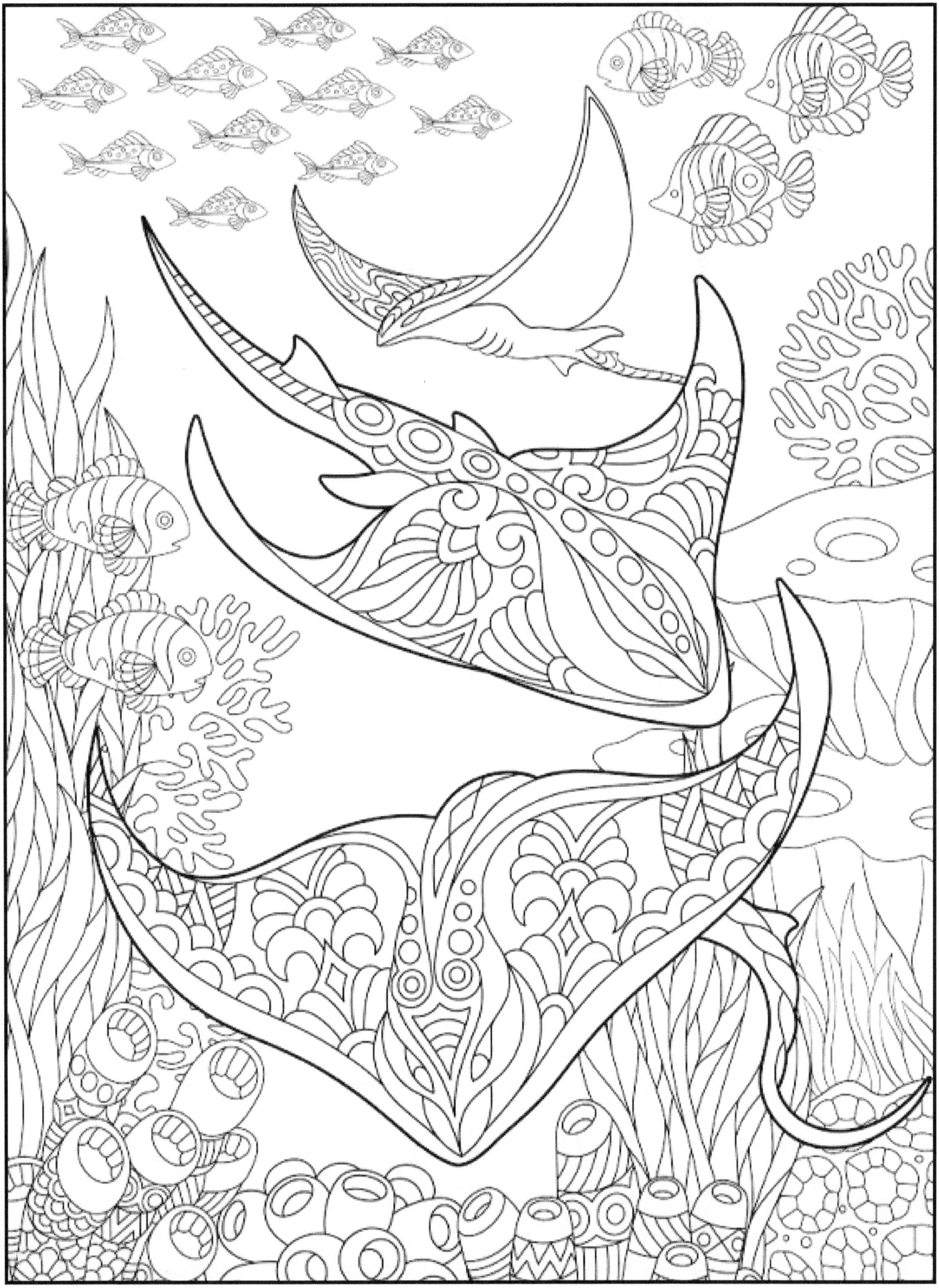

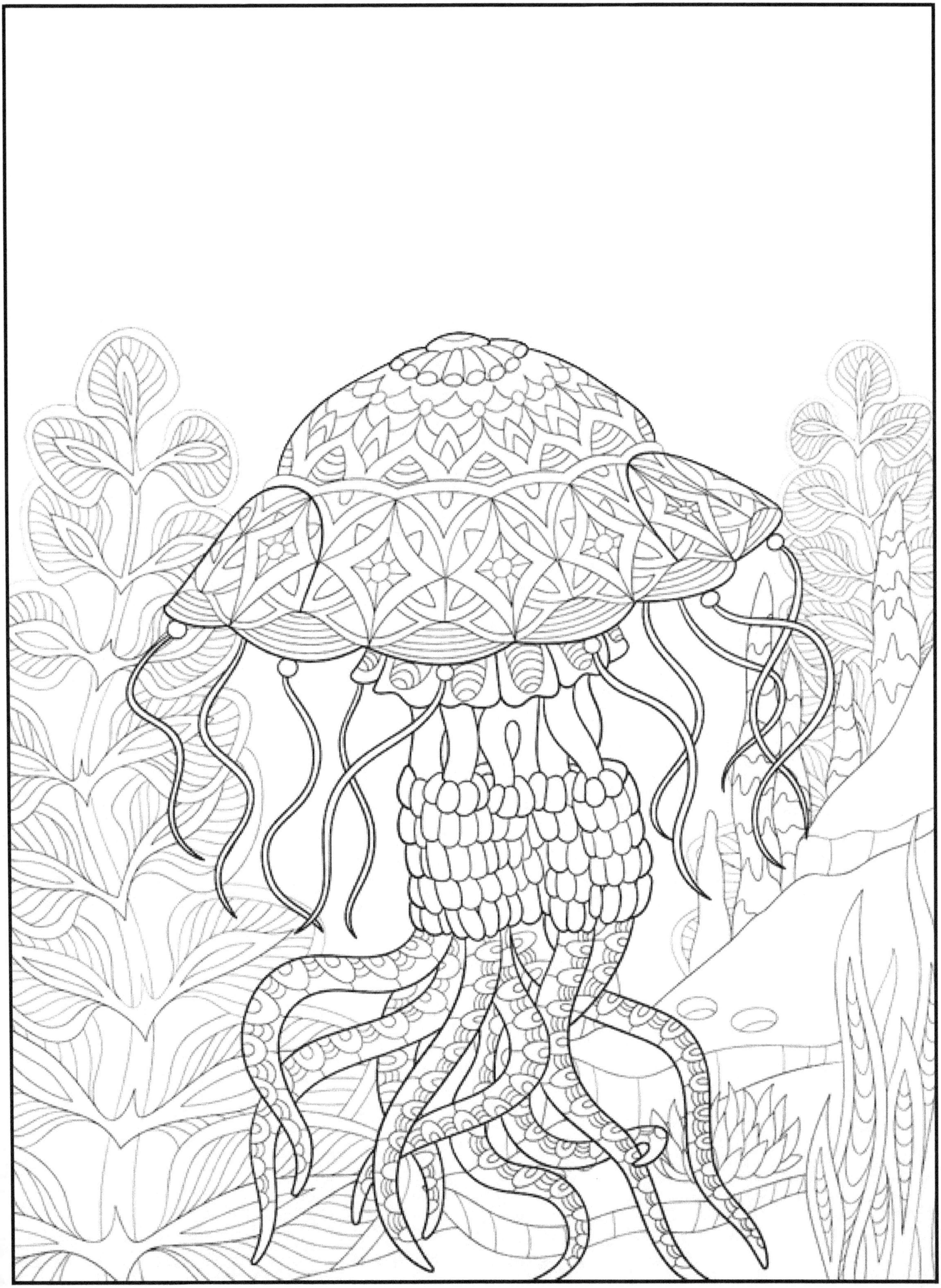

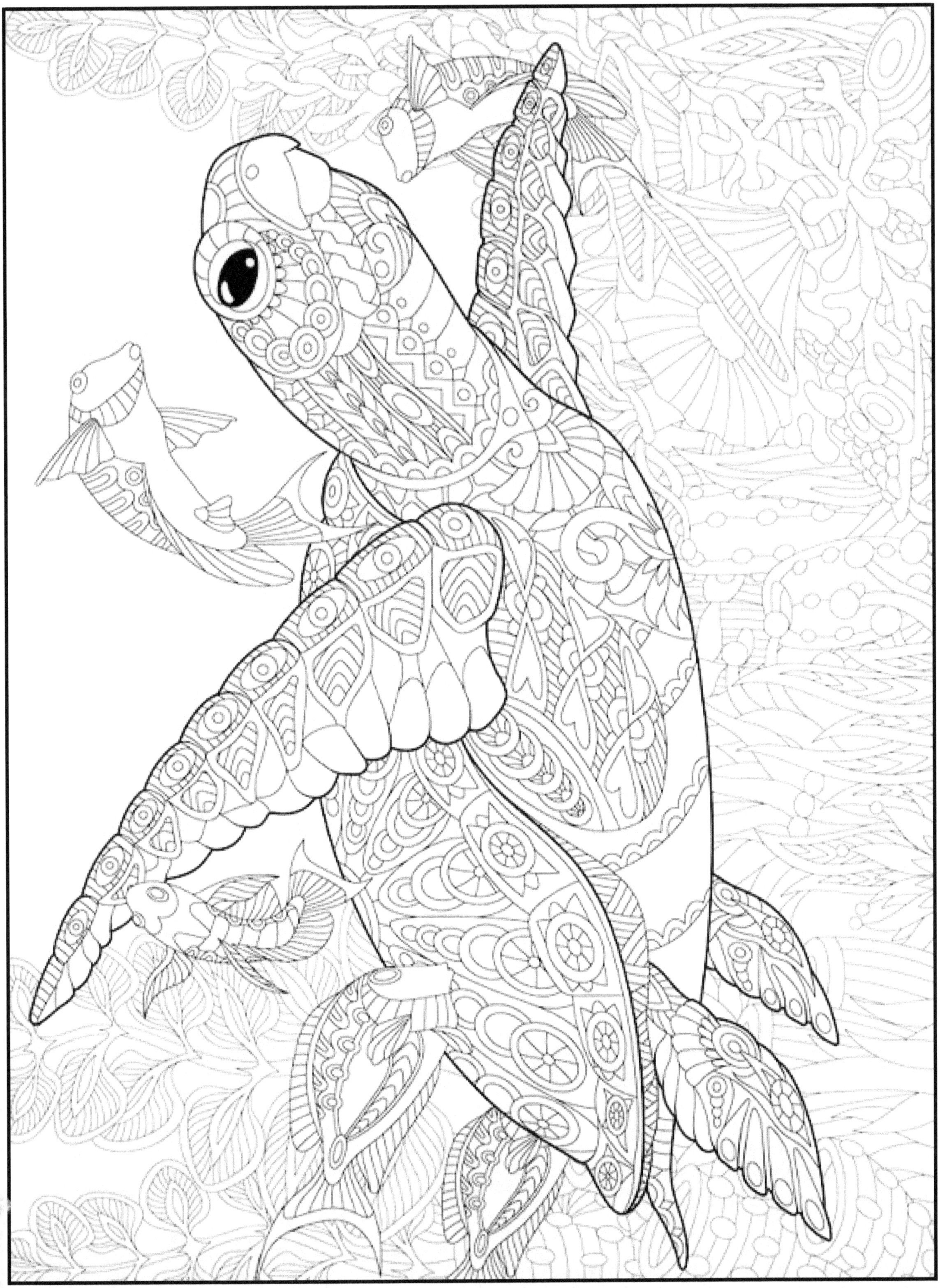

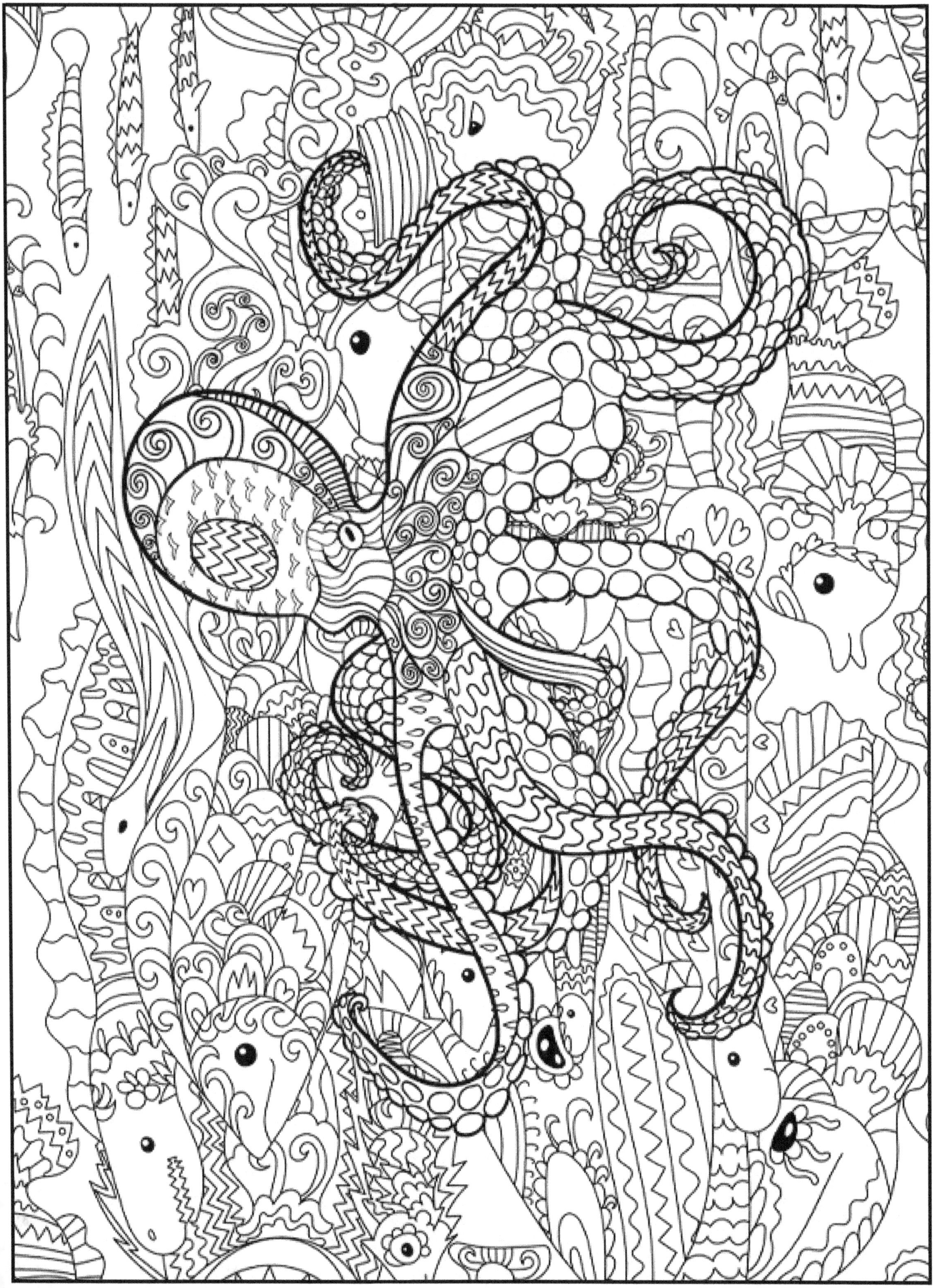

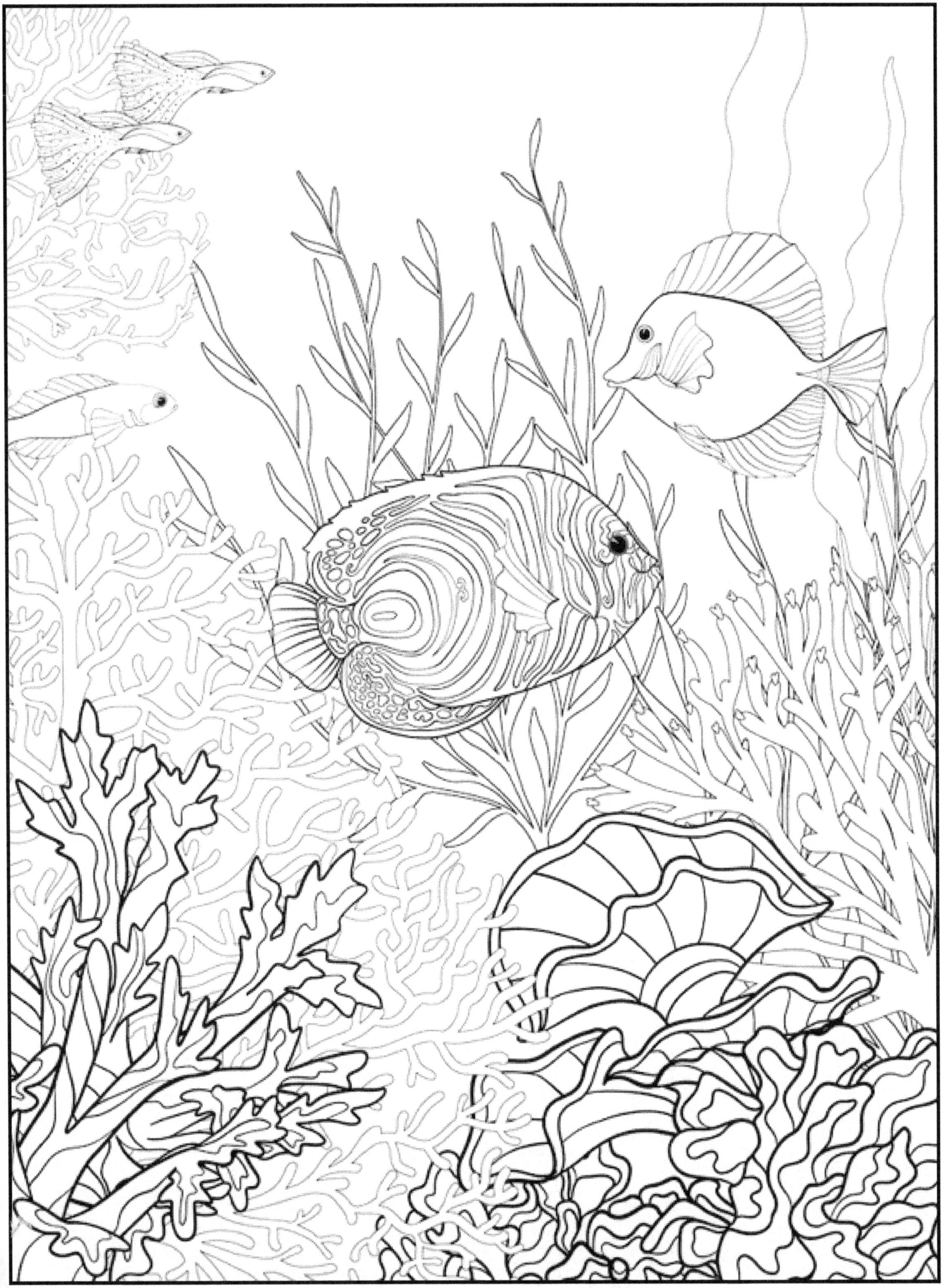

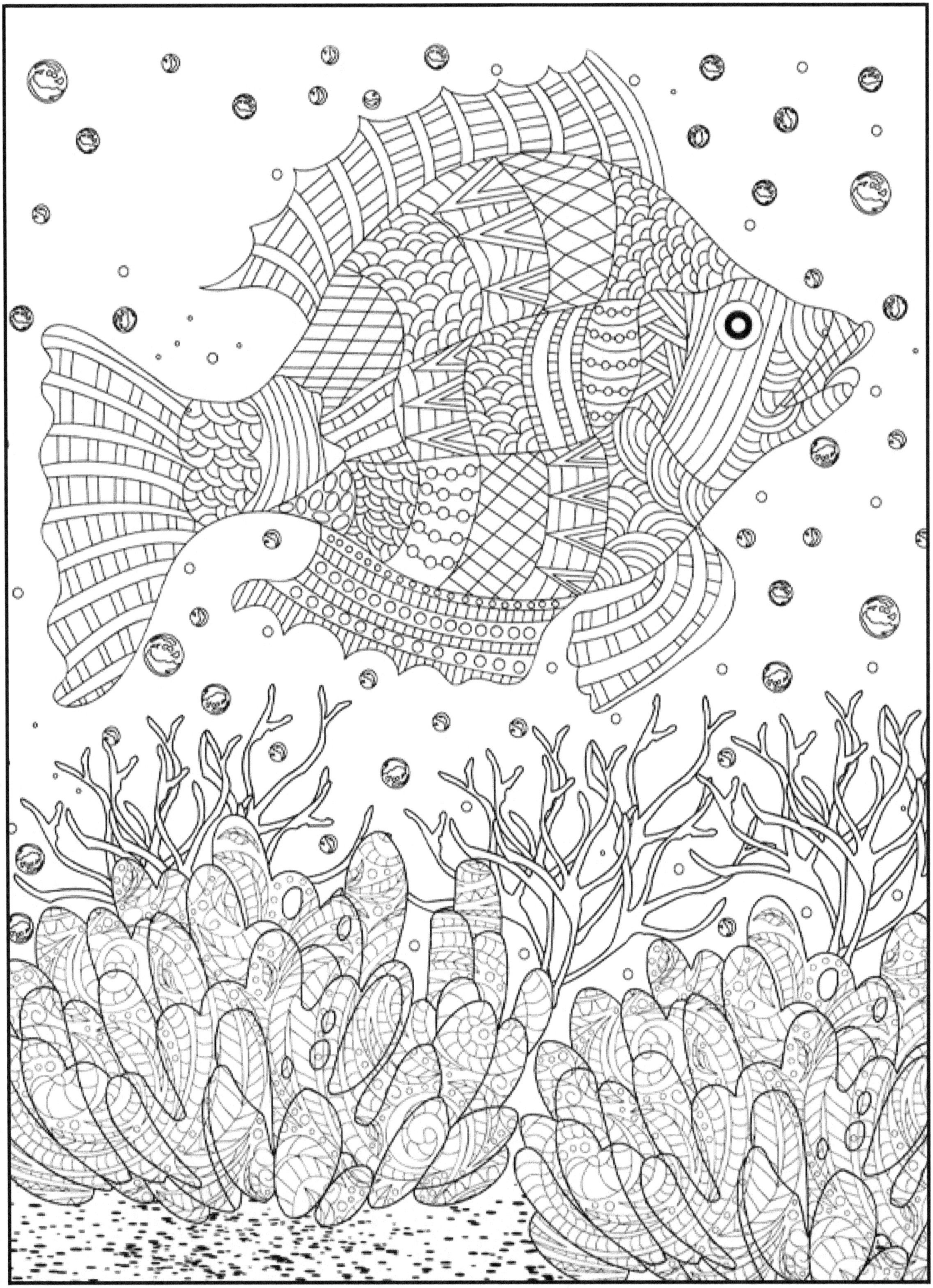

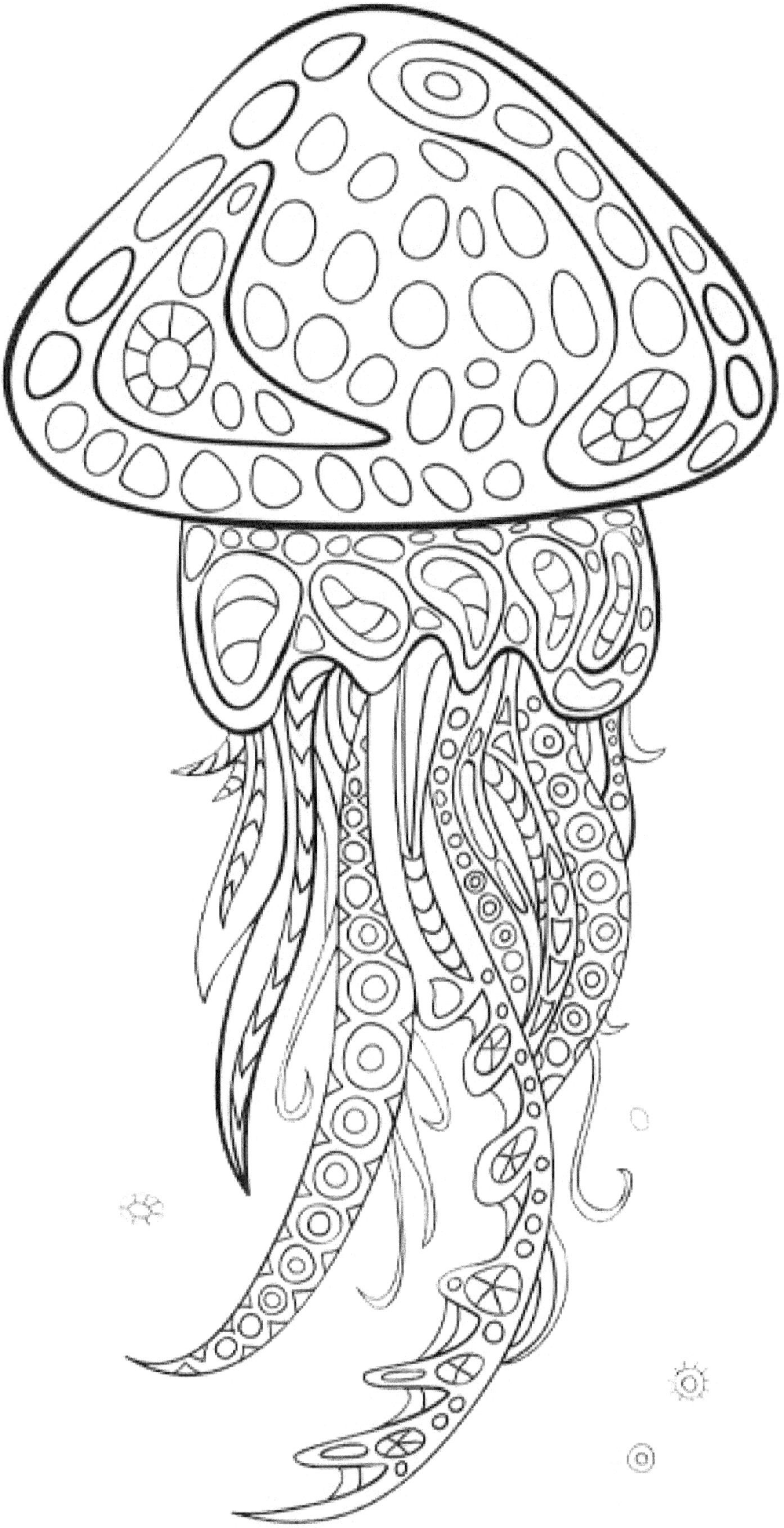

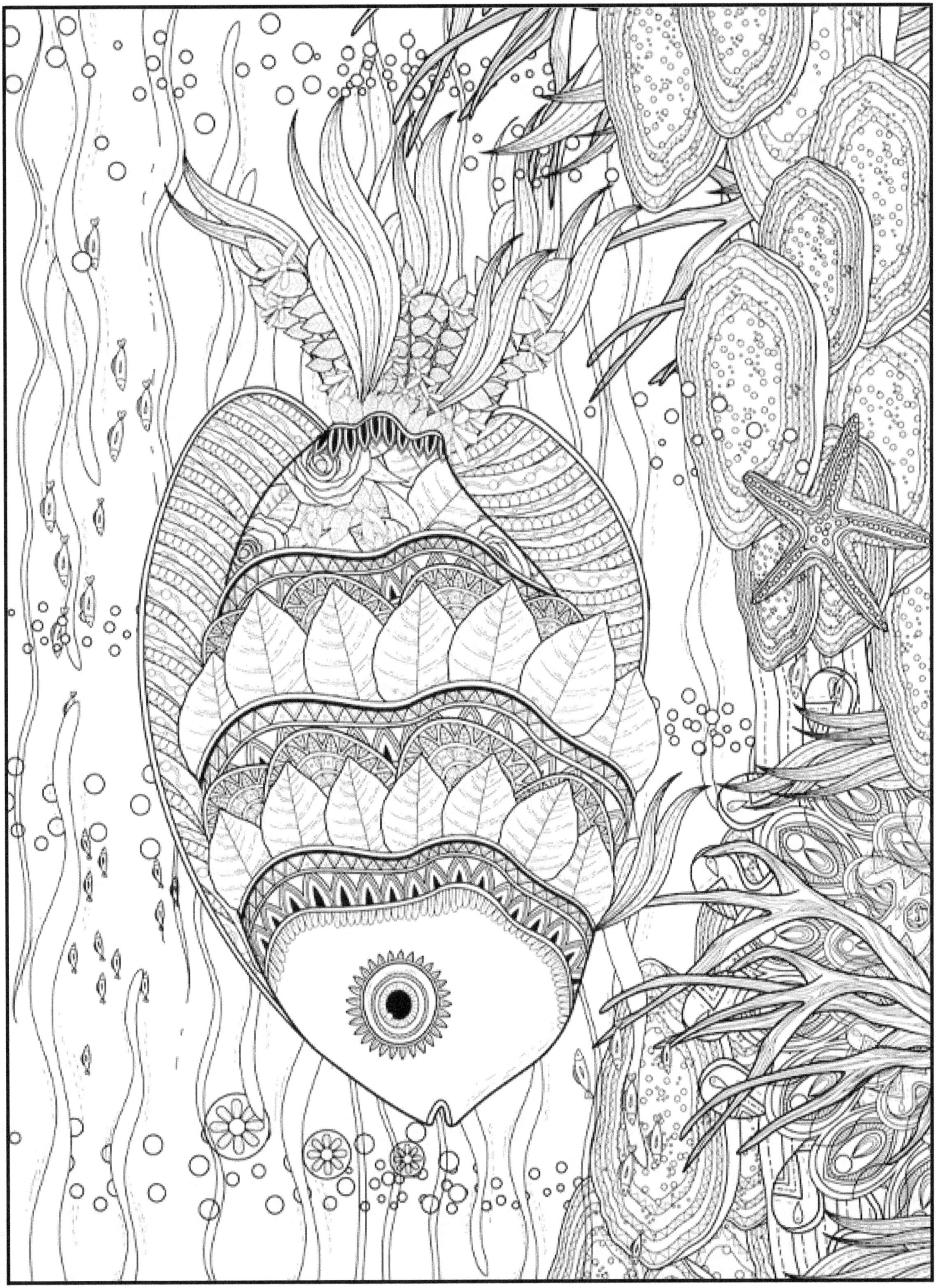

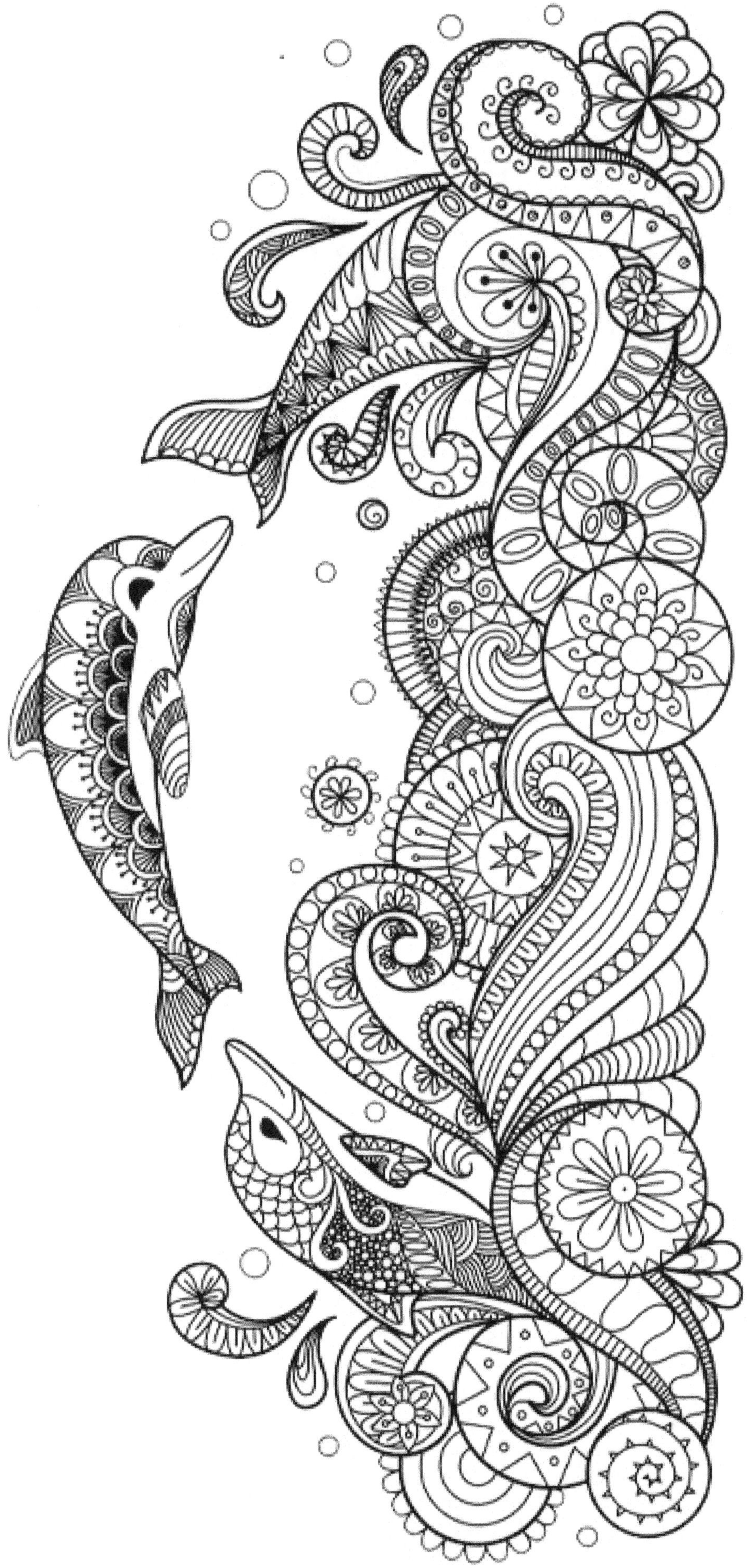

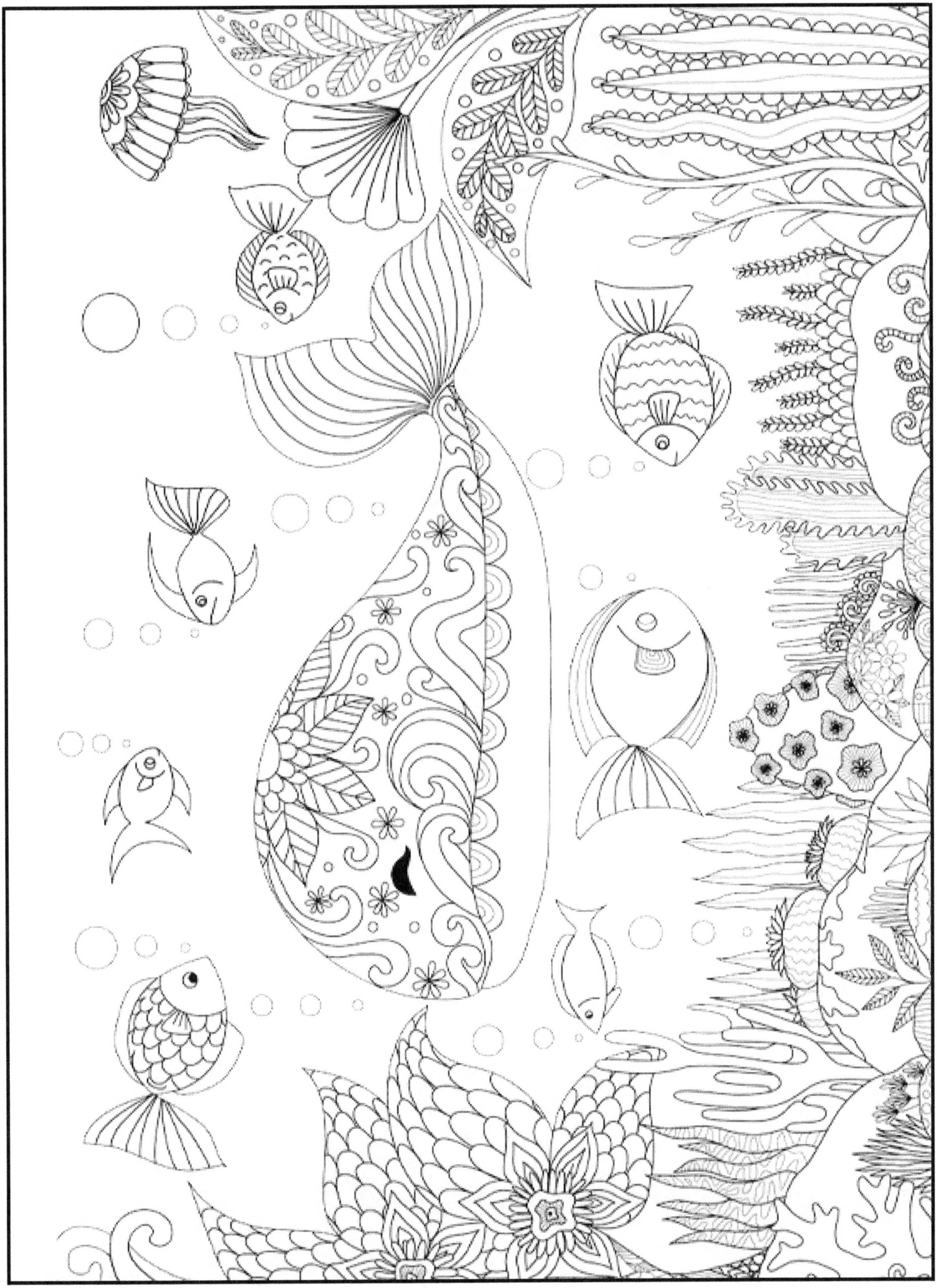

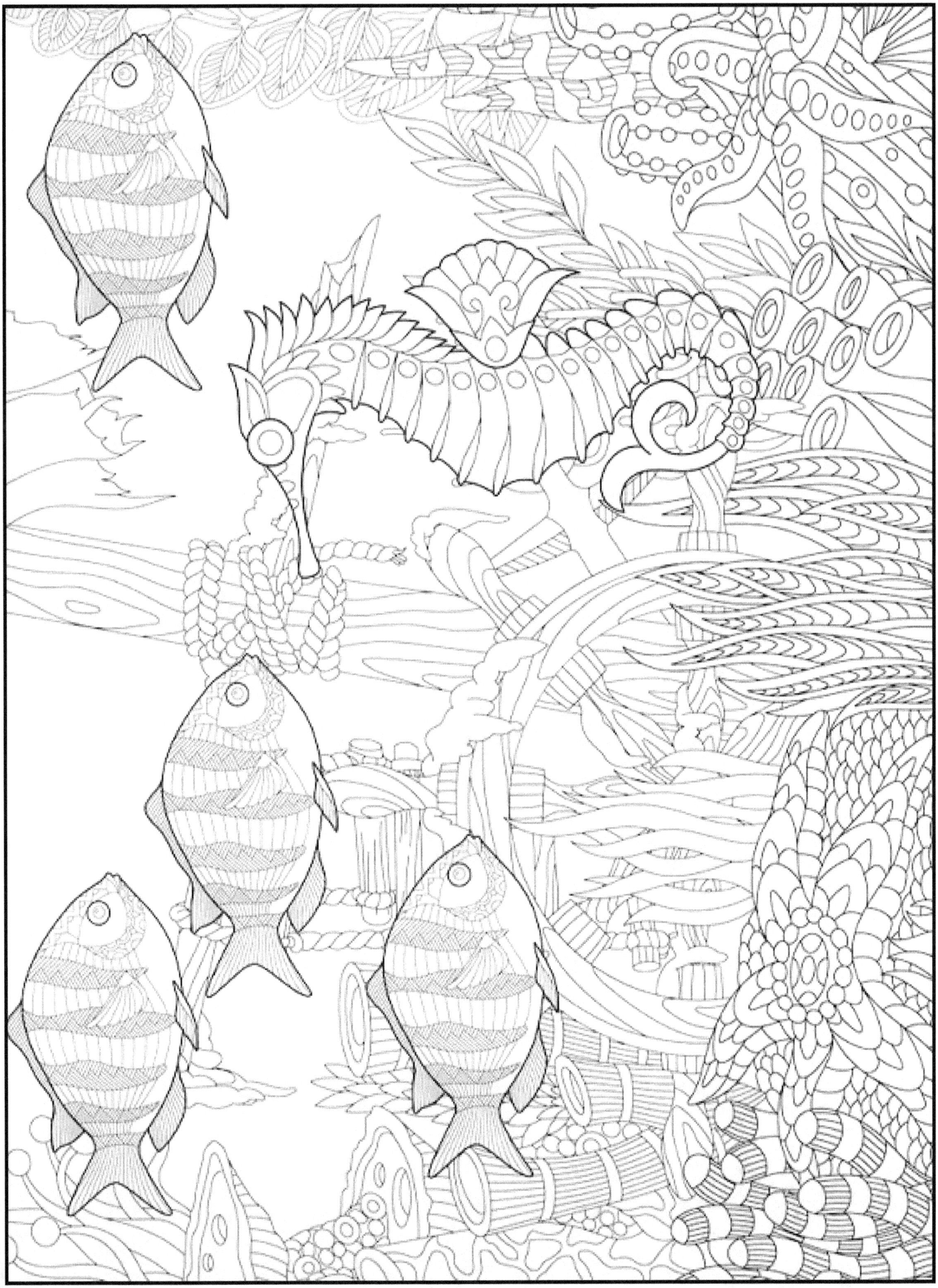

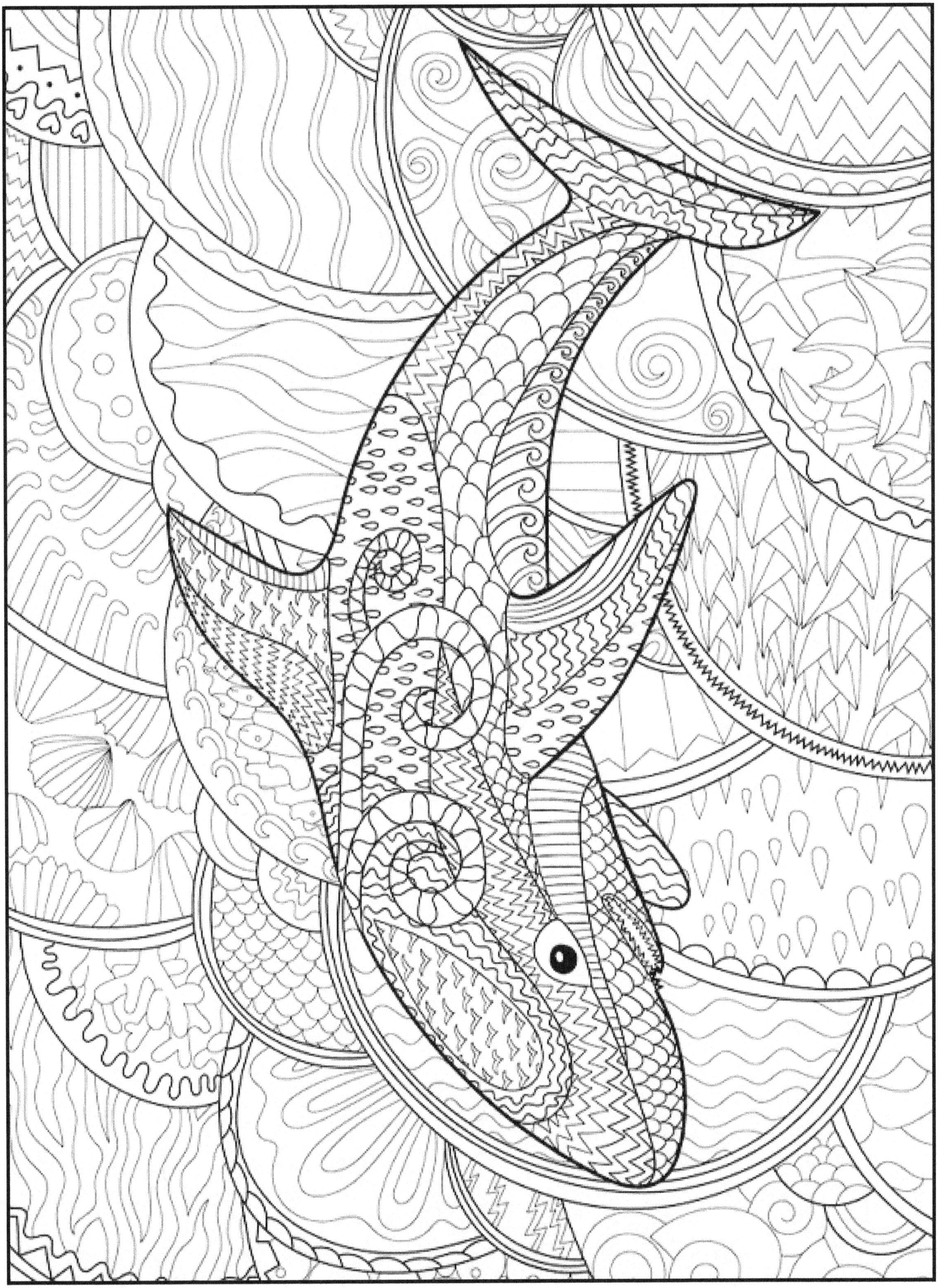

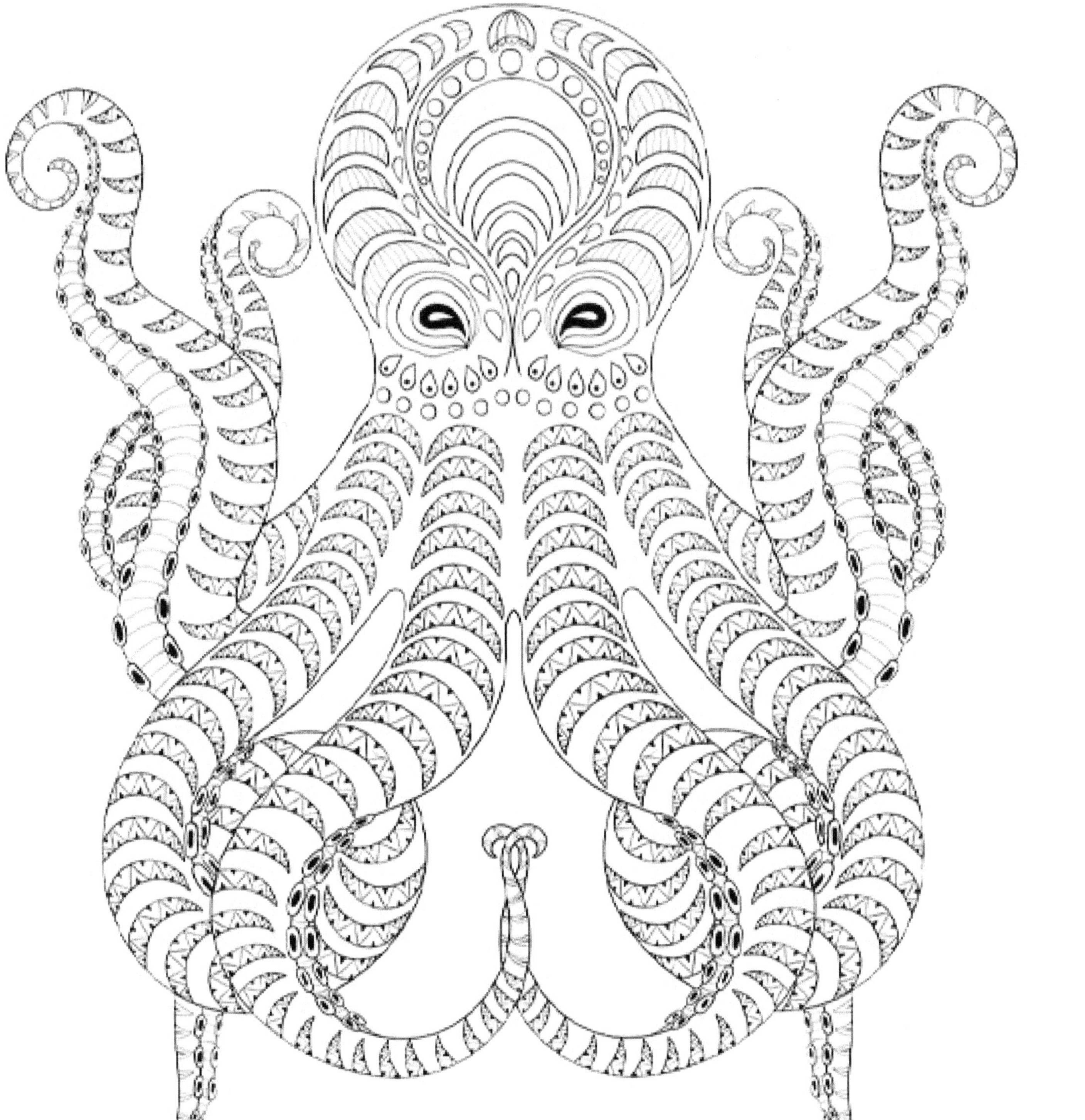

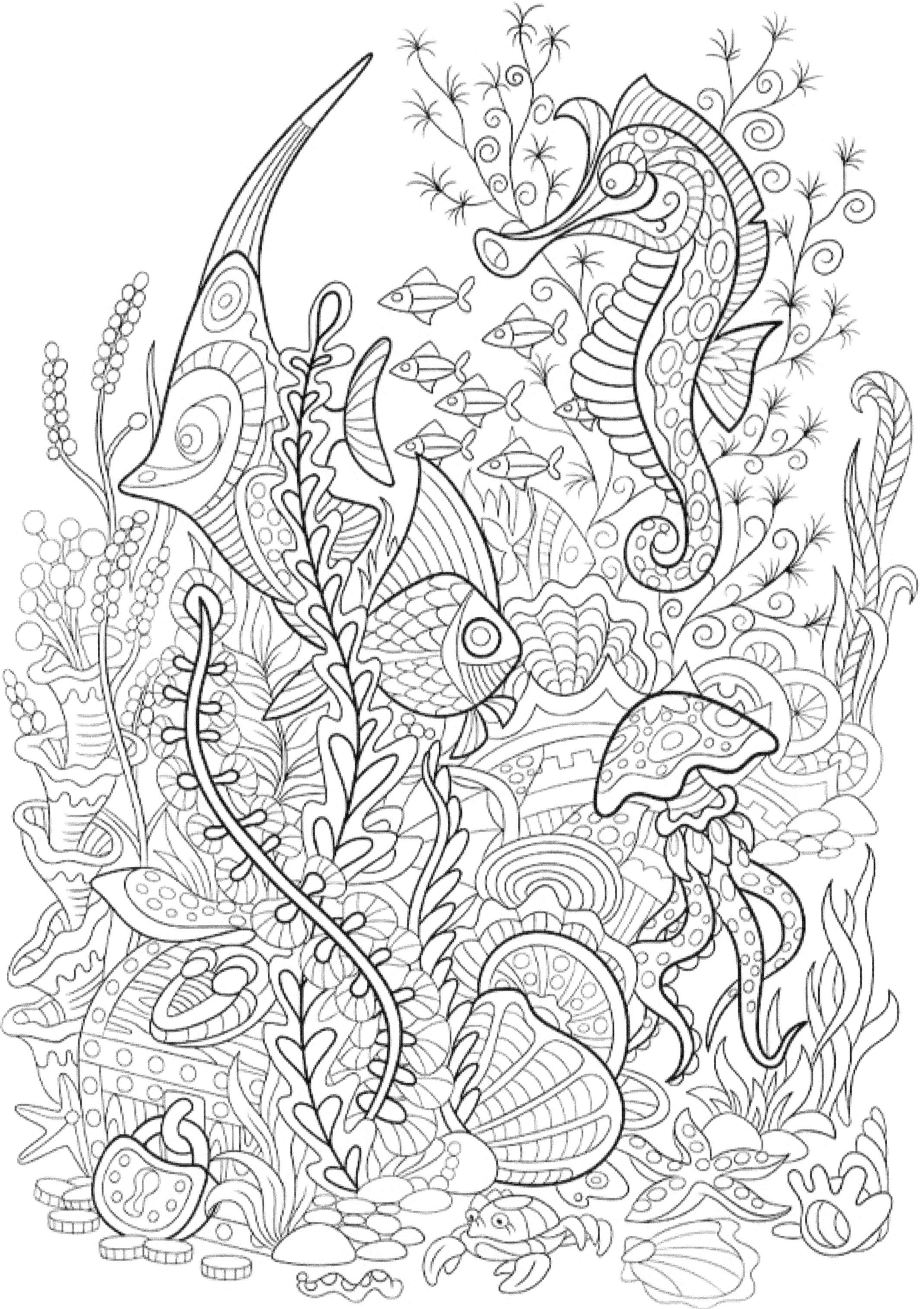

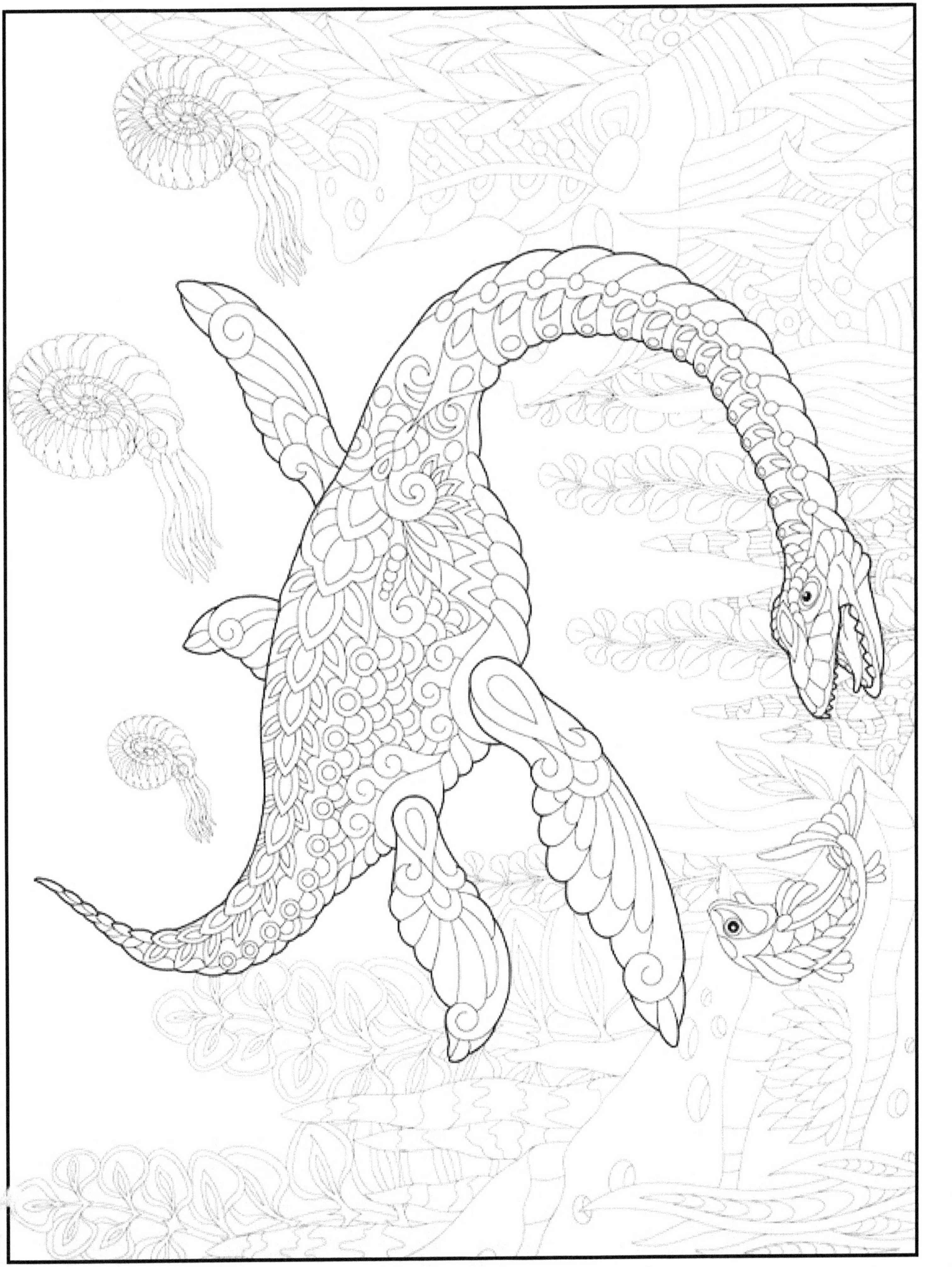

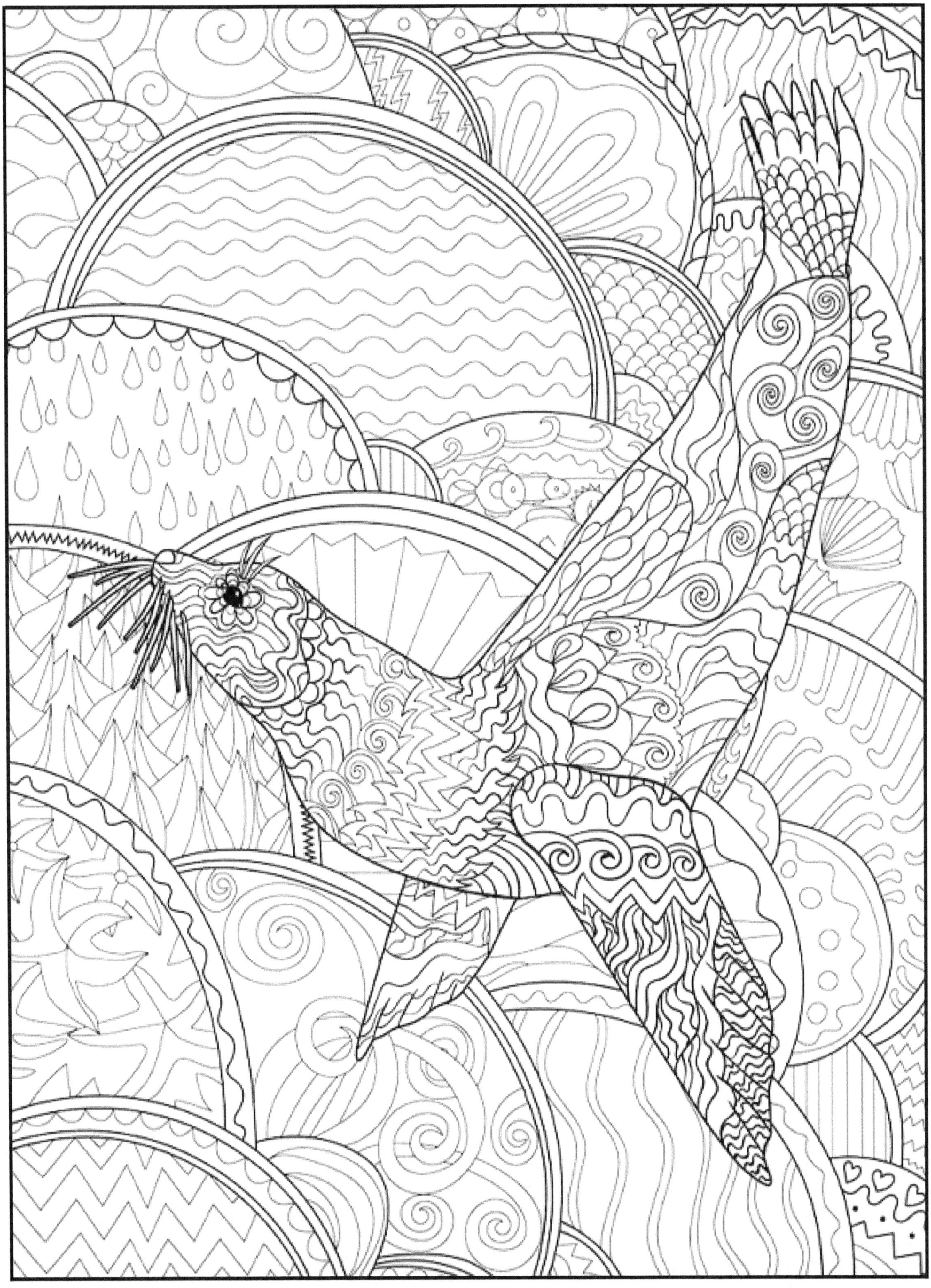

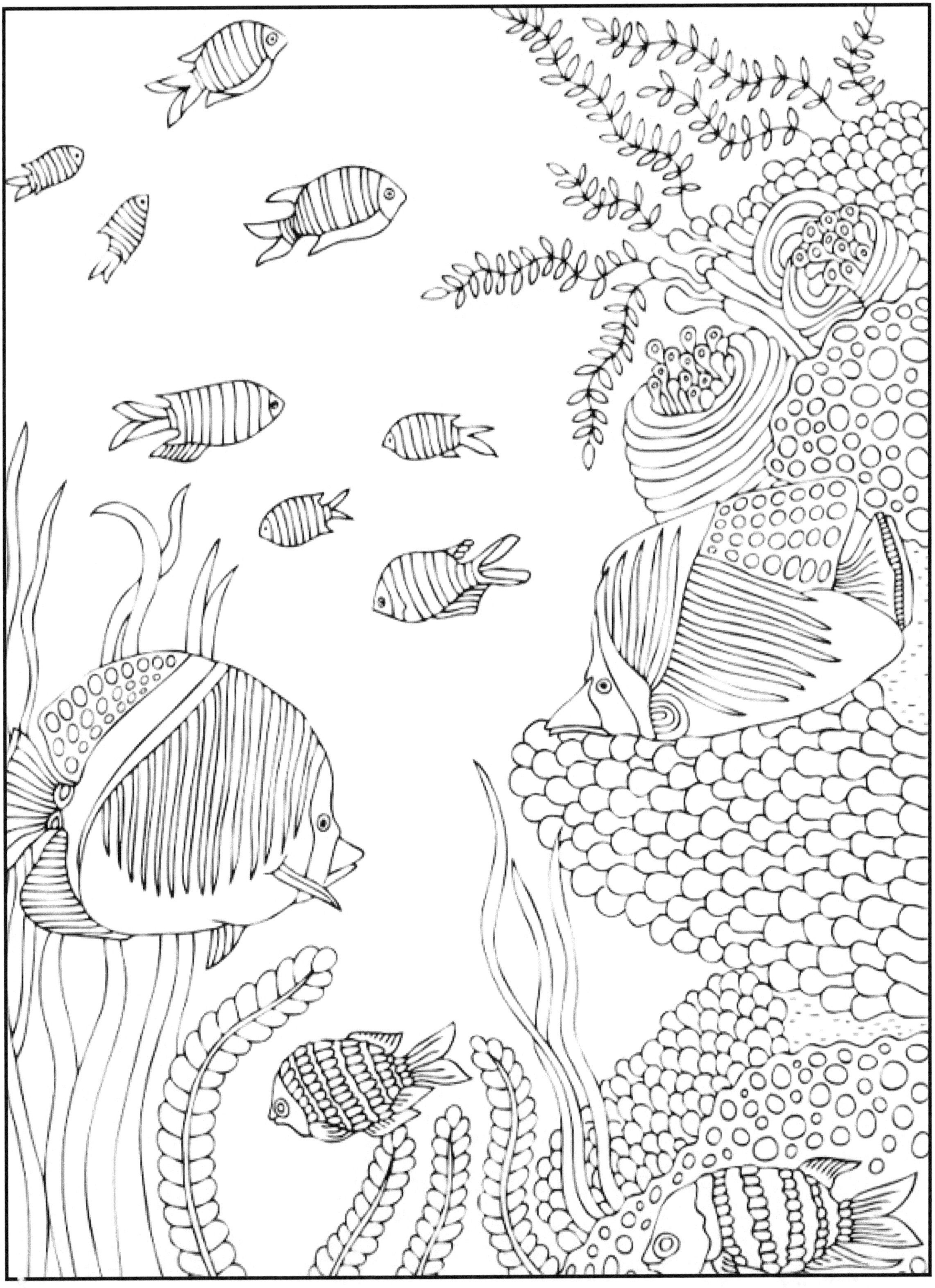

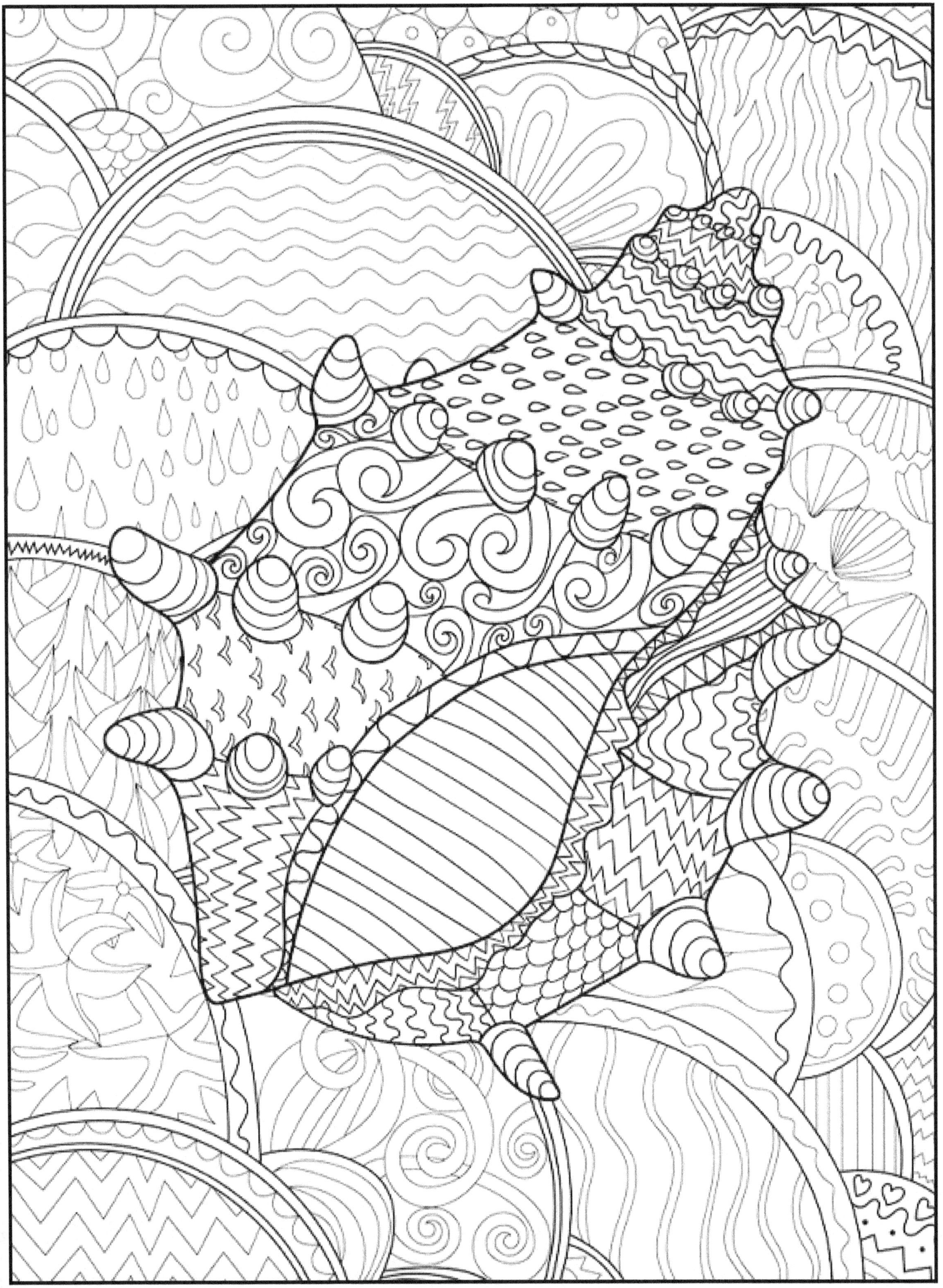

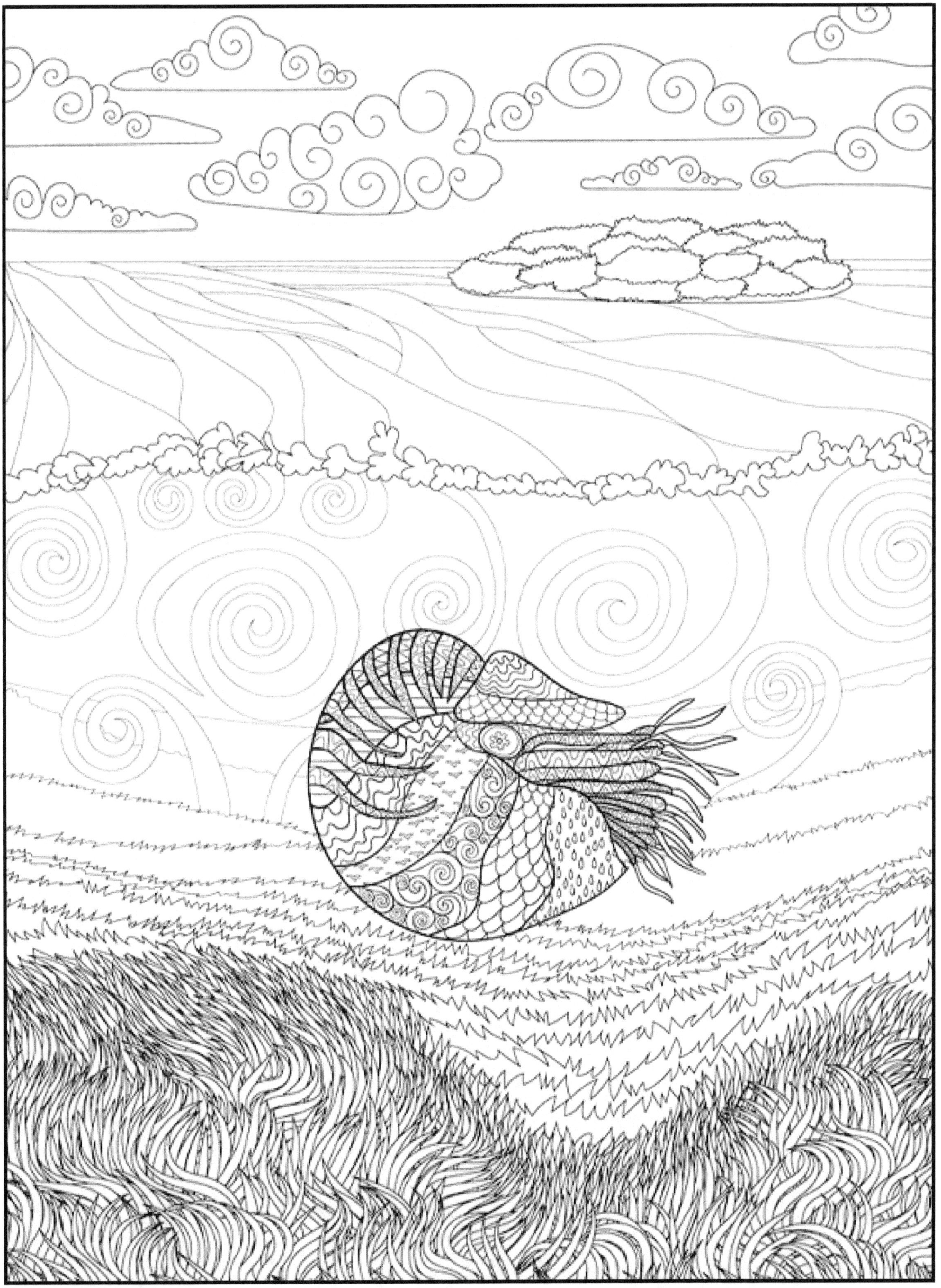

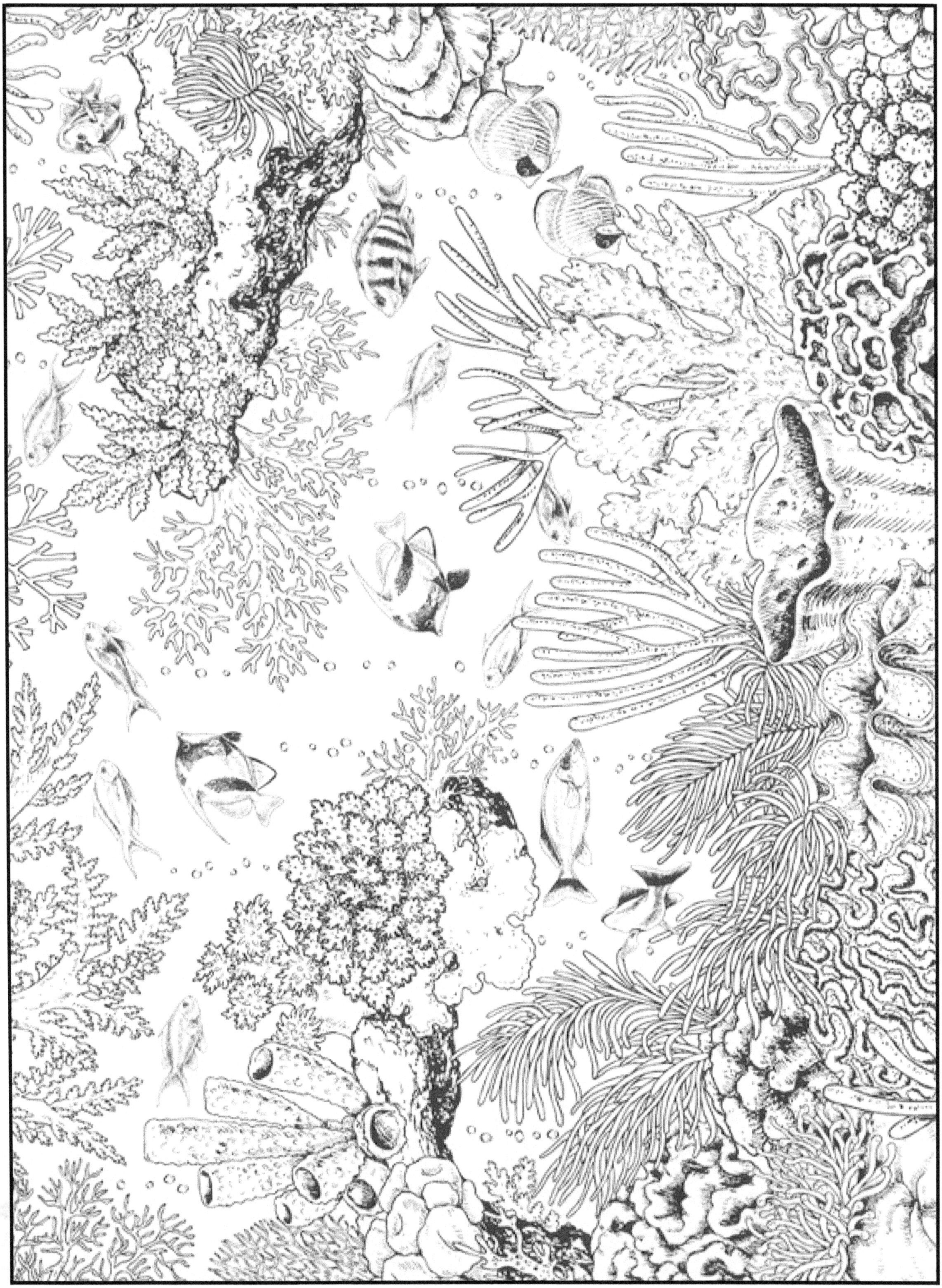

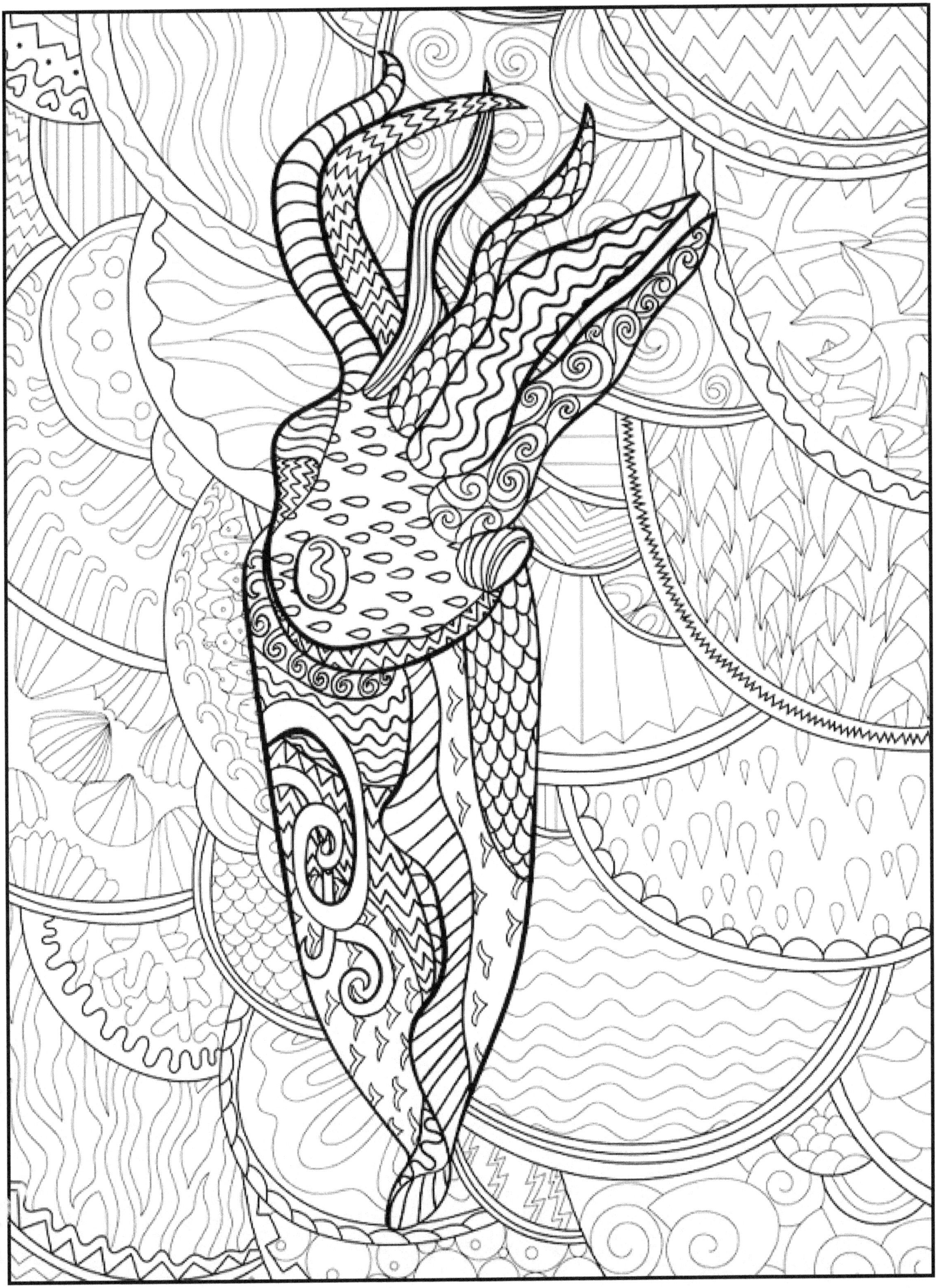

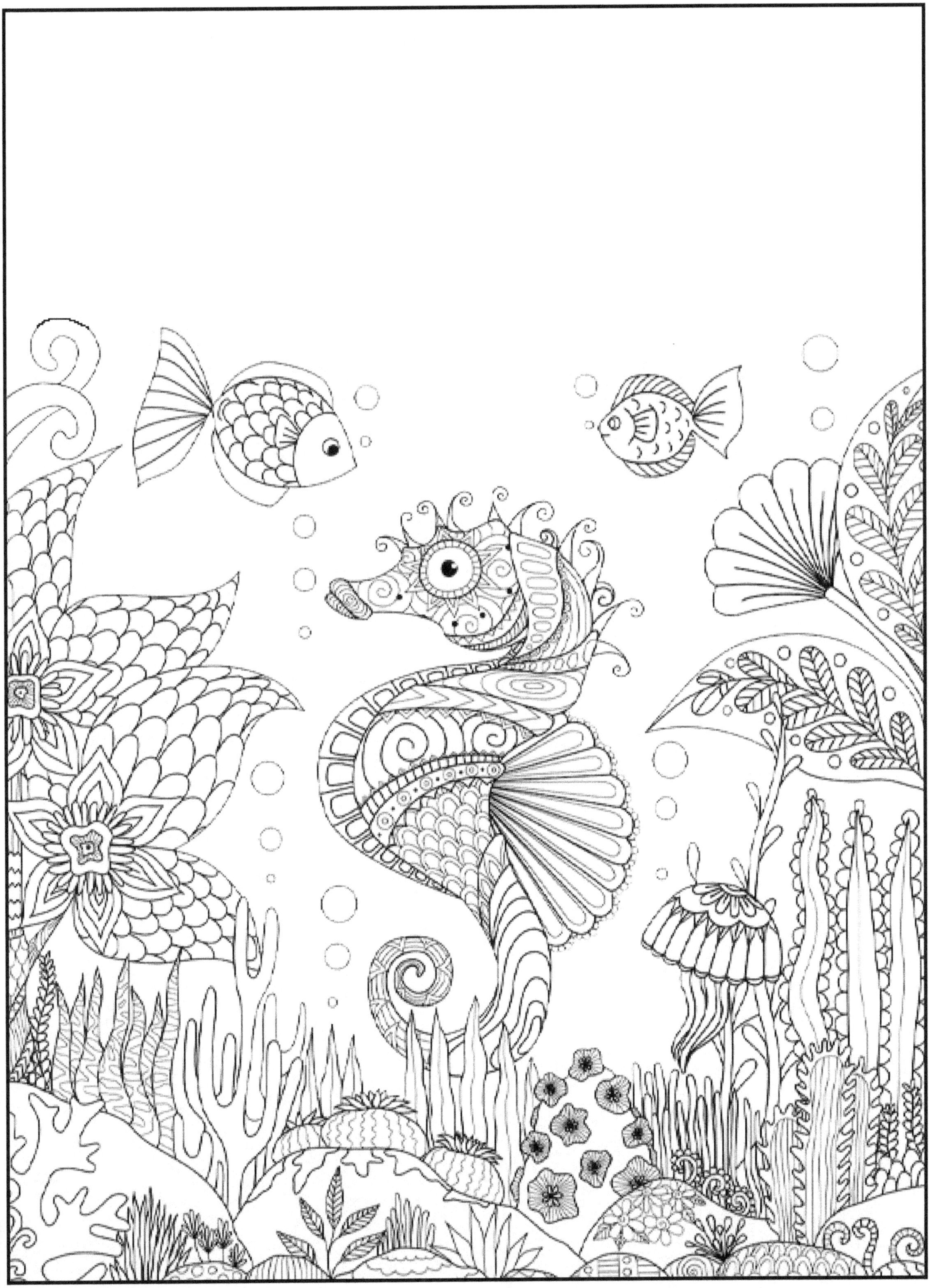

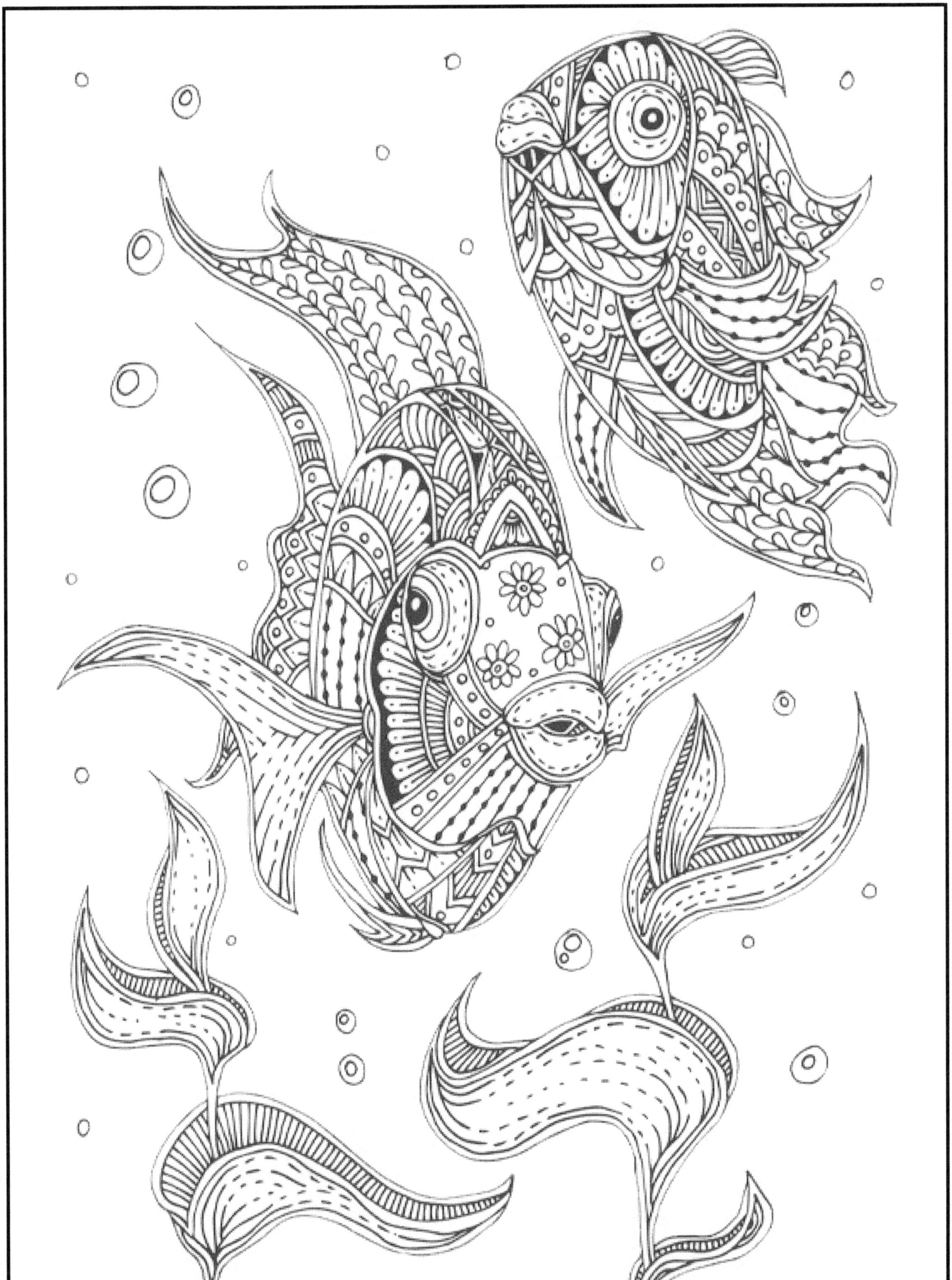

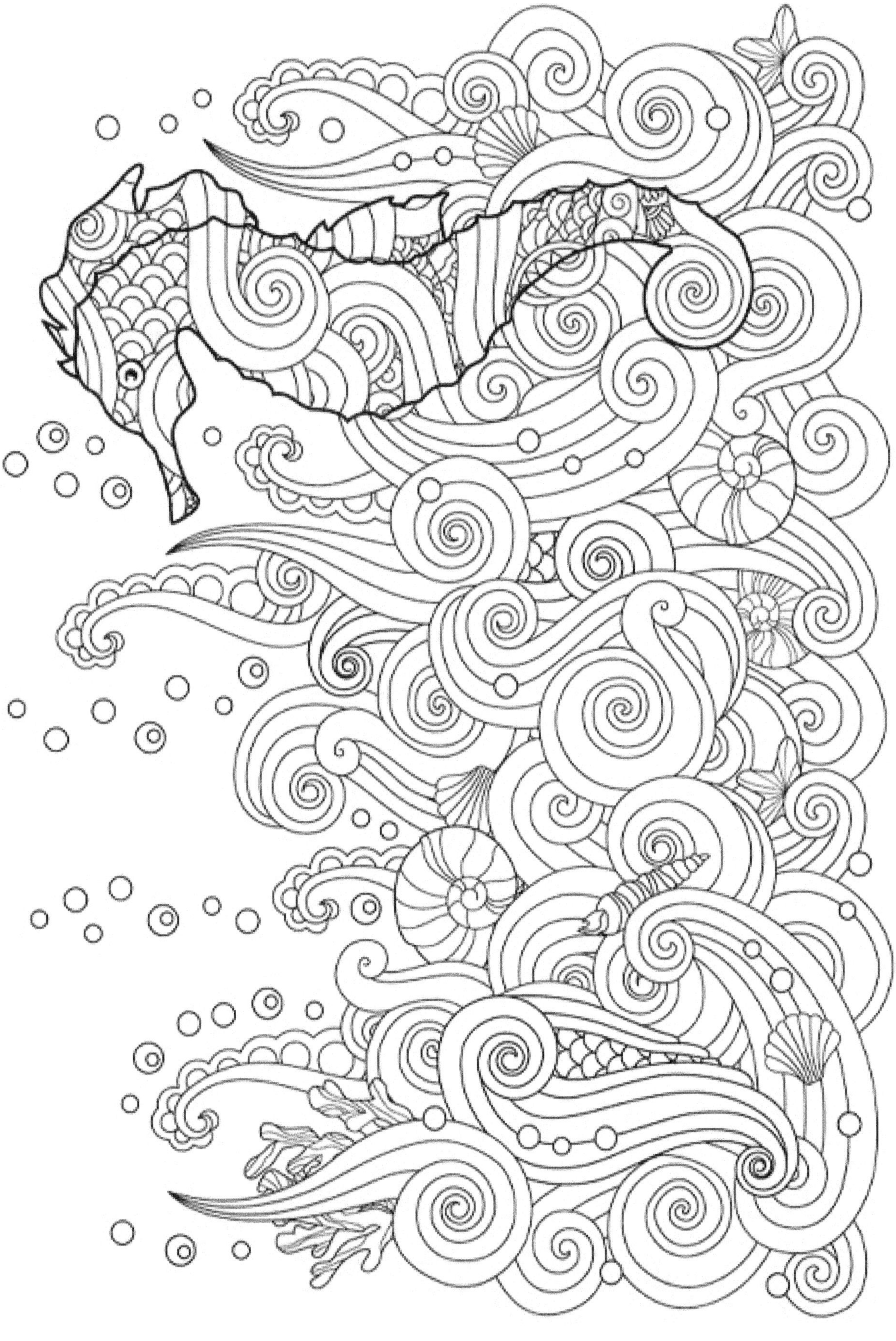

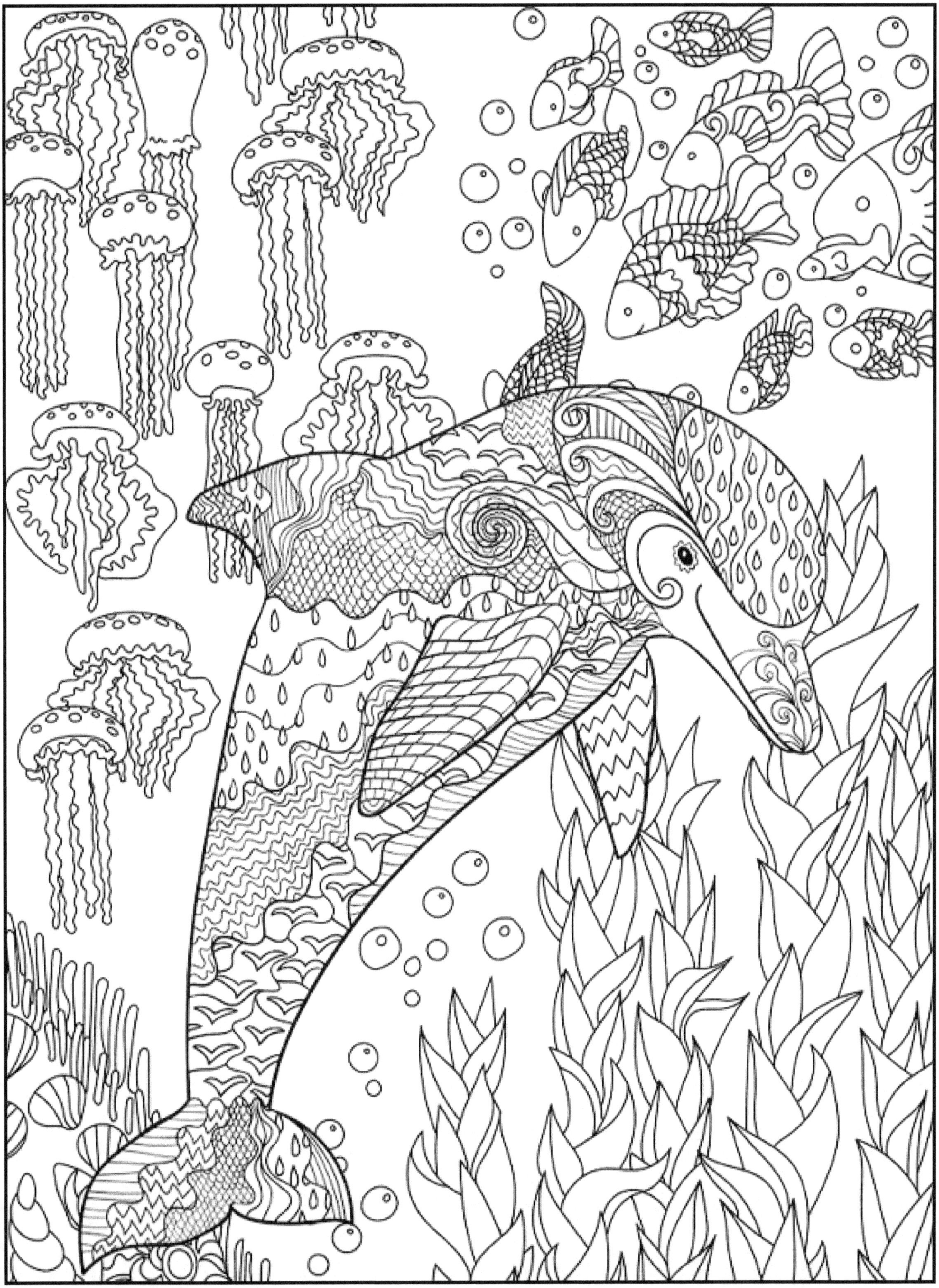

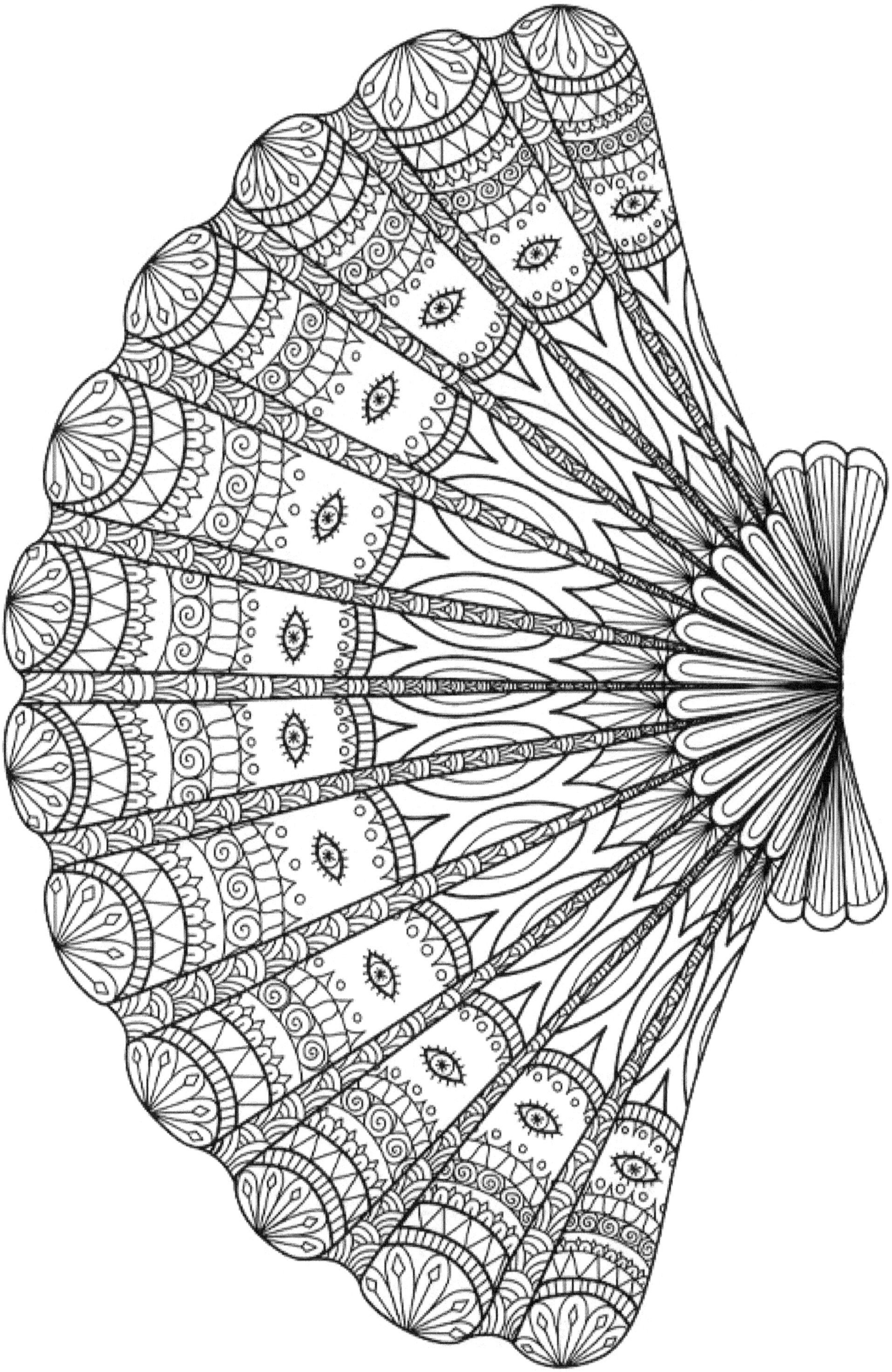

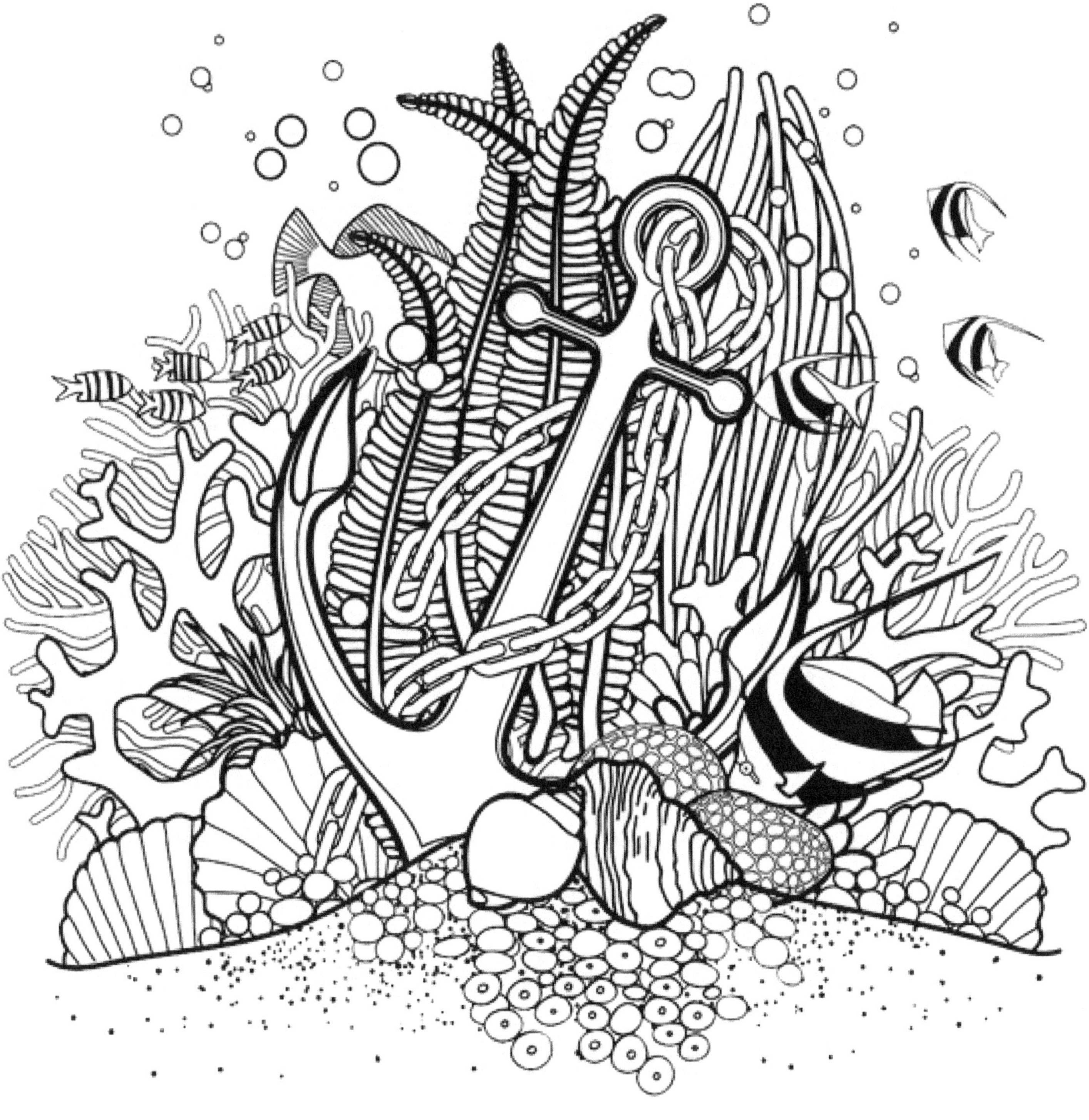

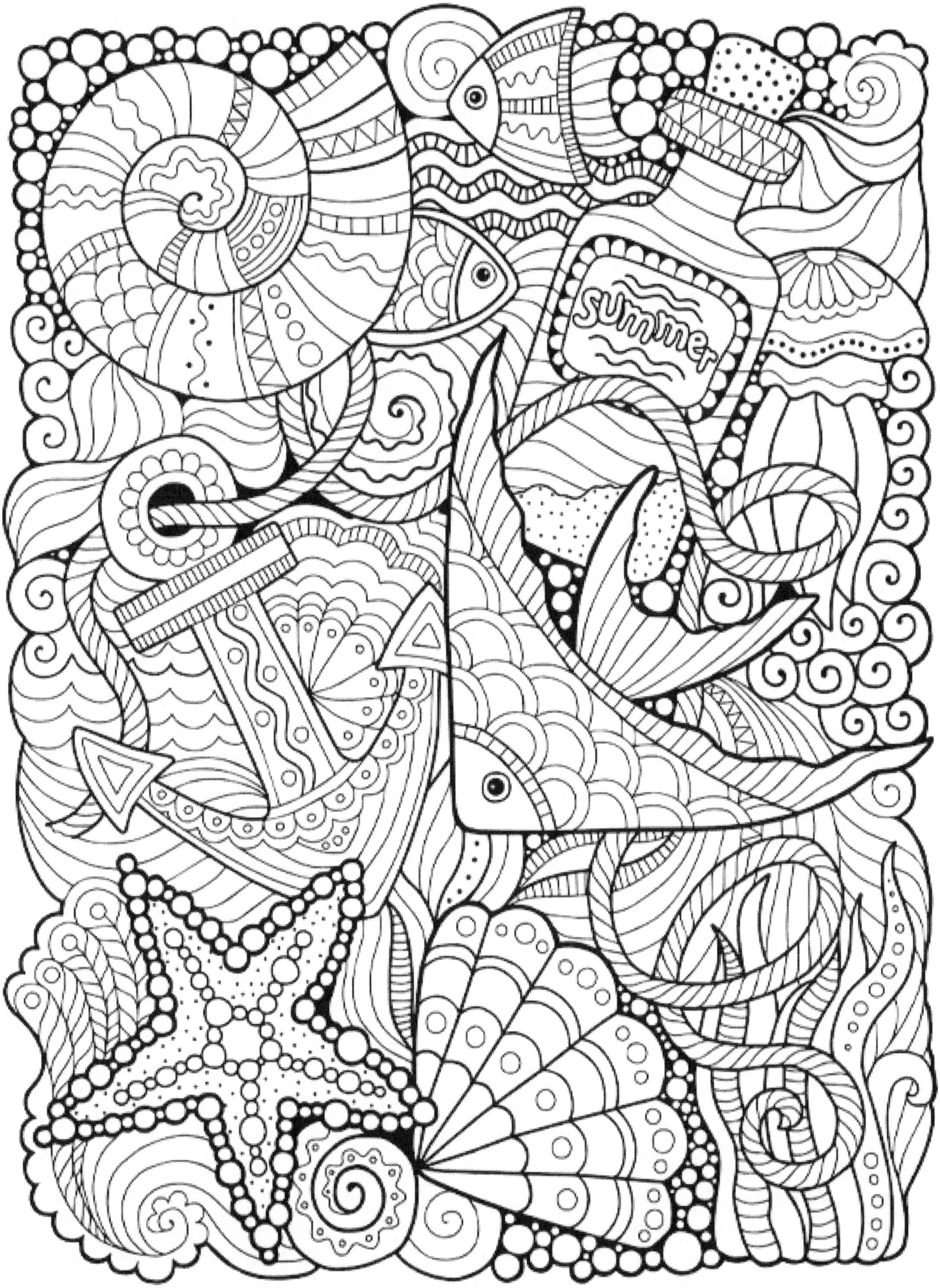
SUMMER

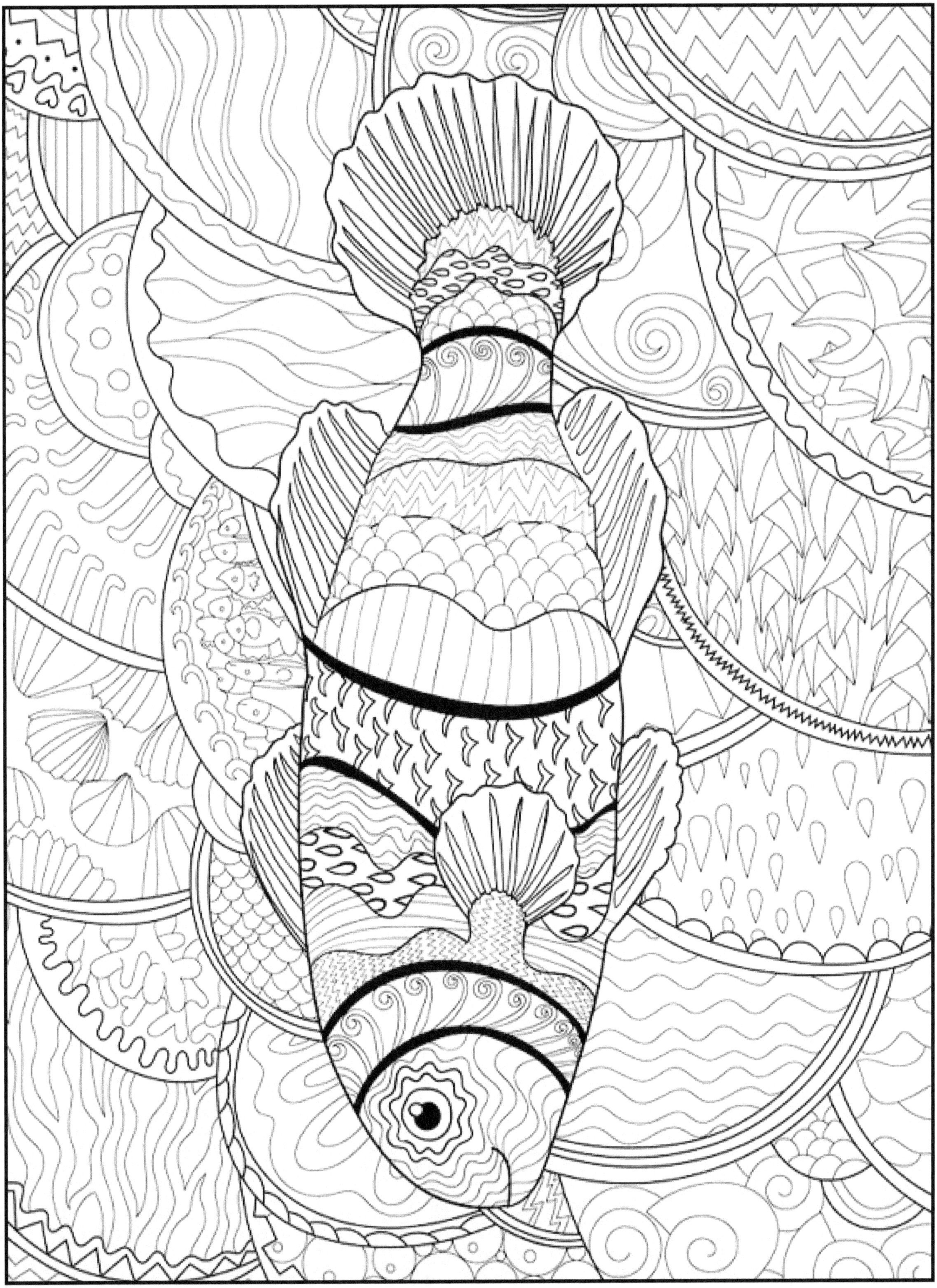

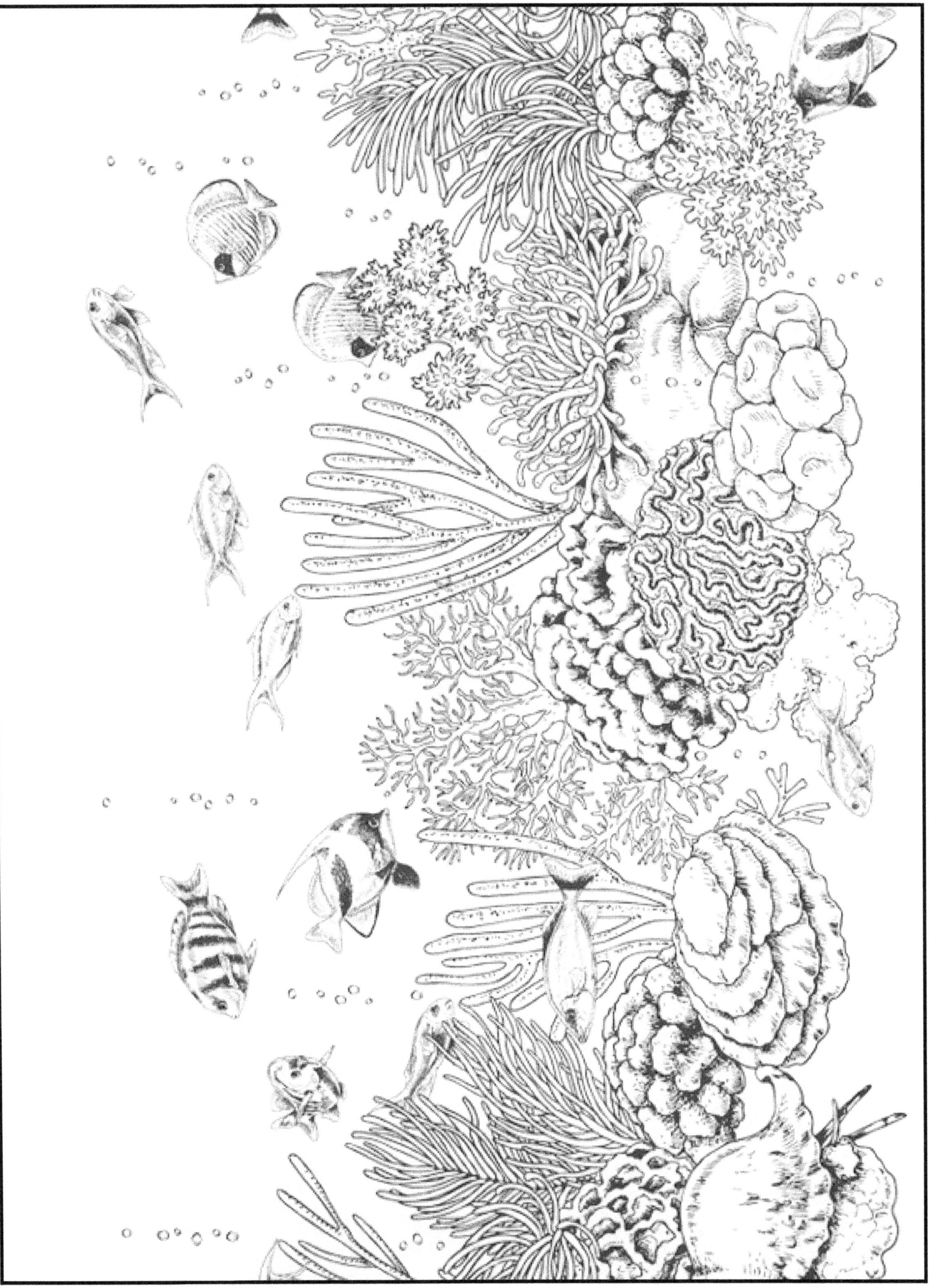

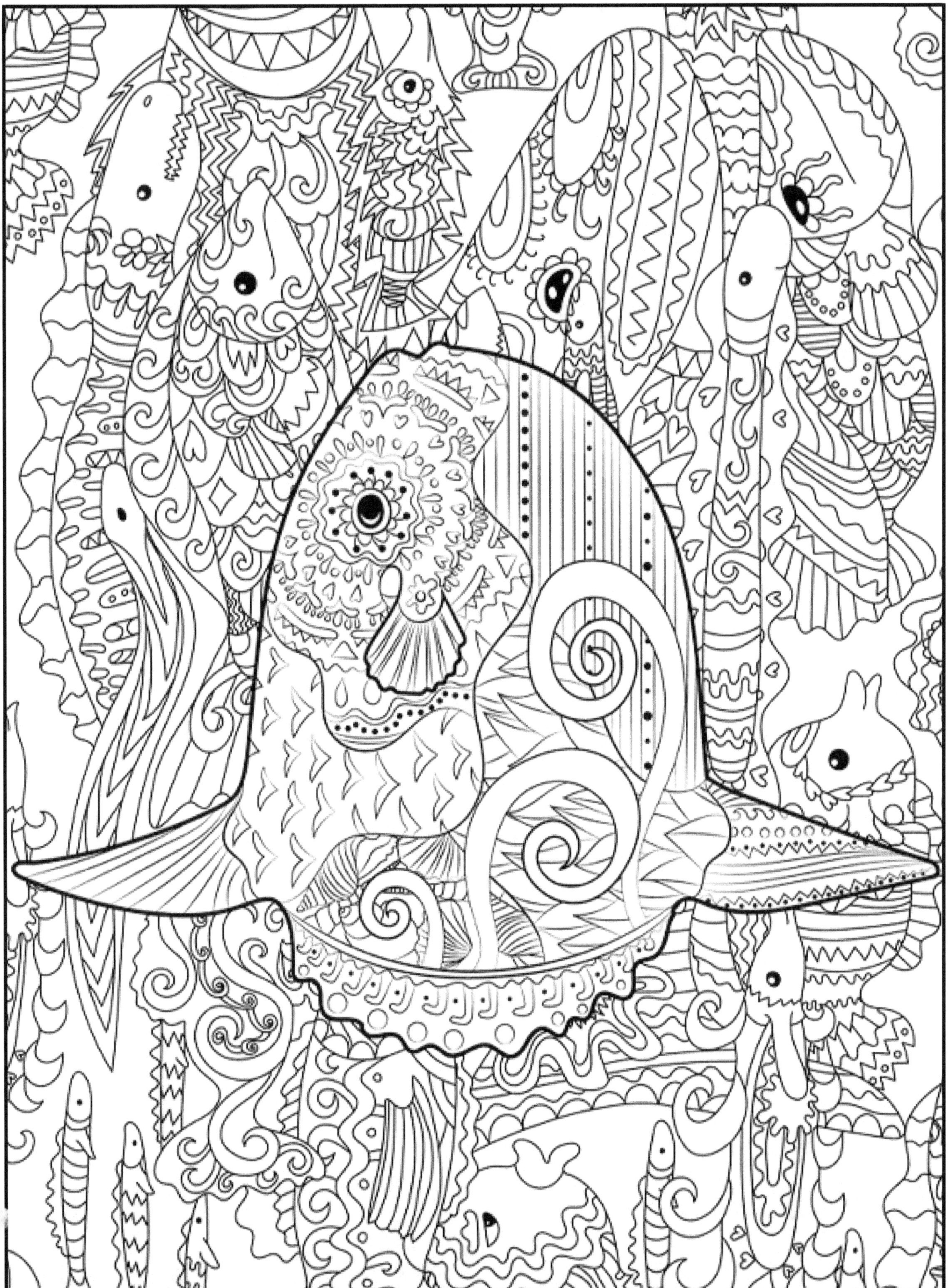

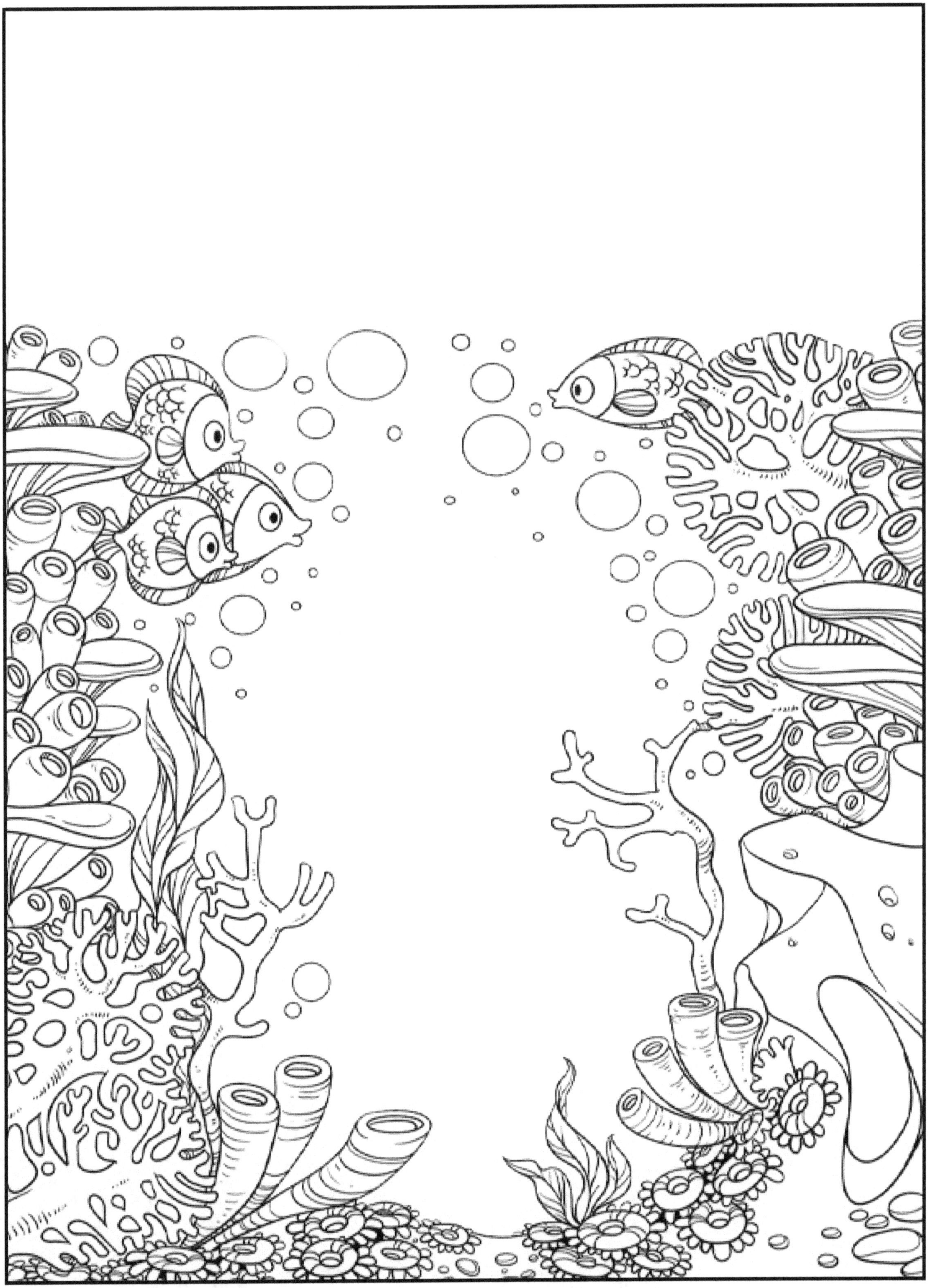

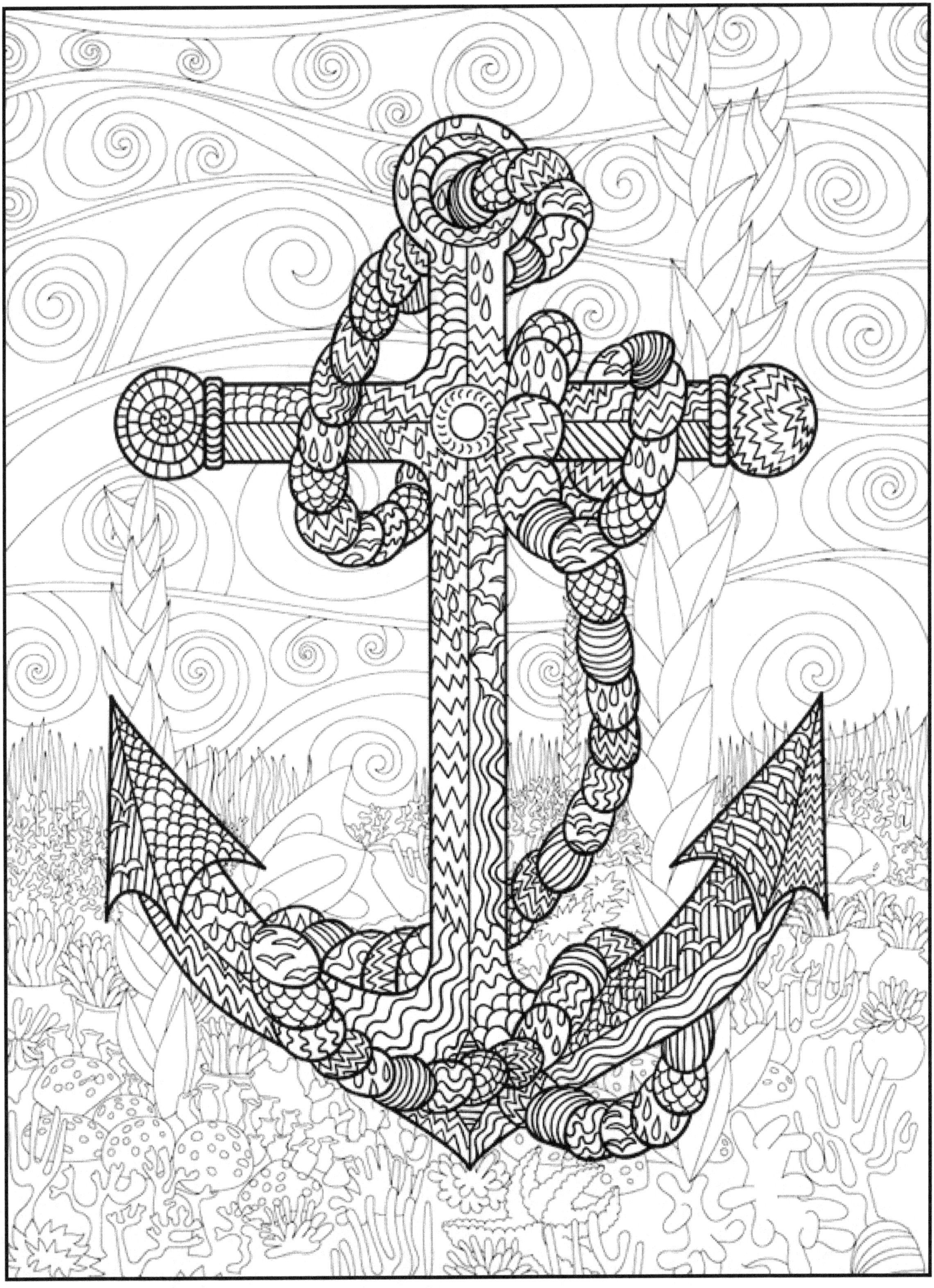

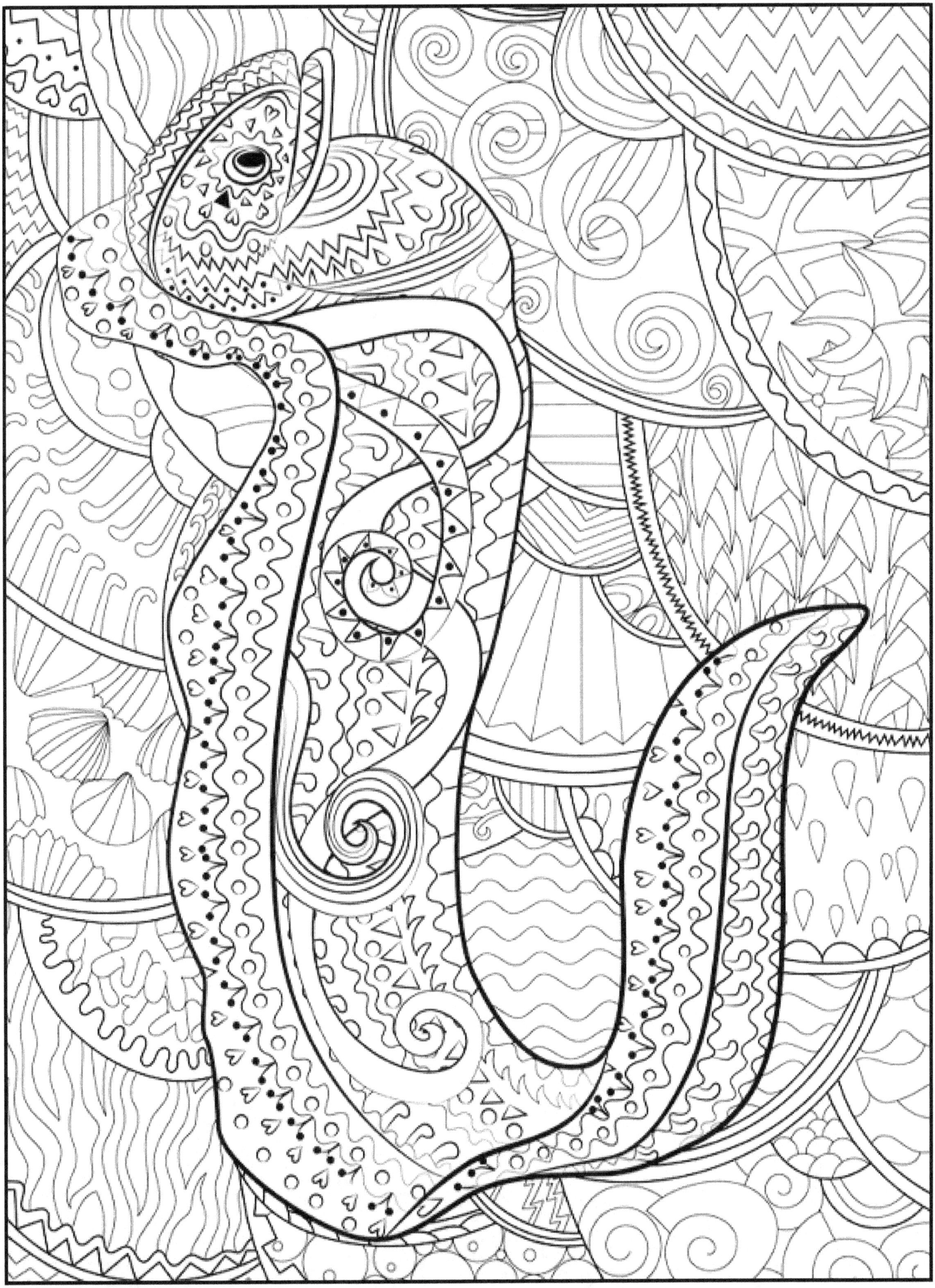

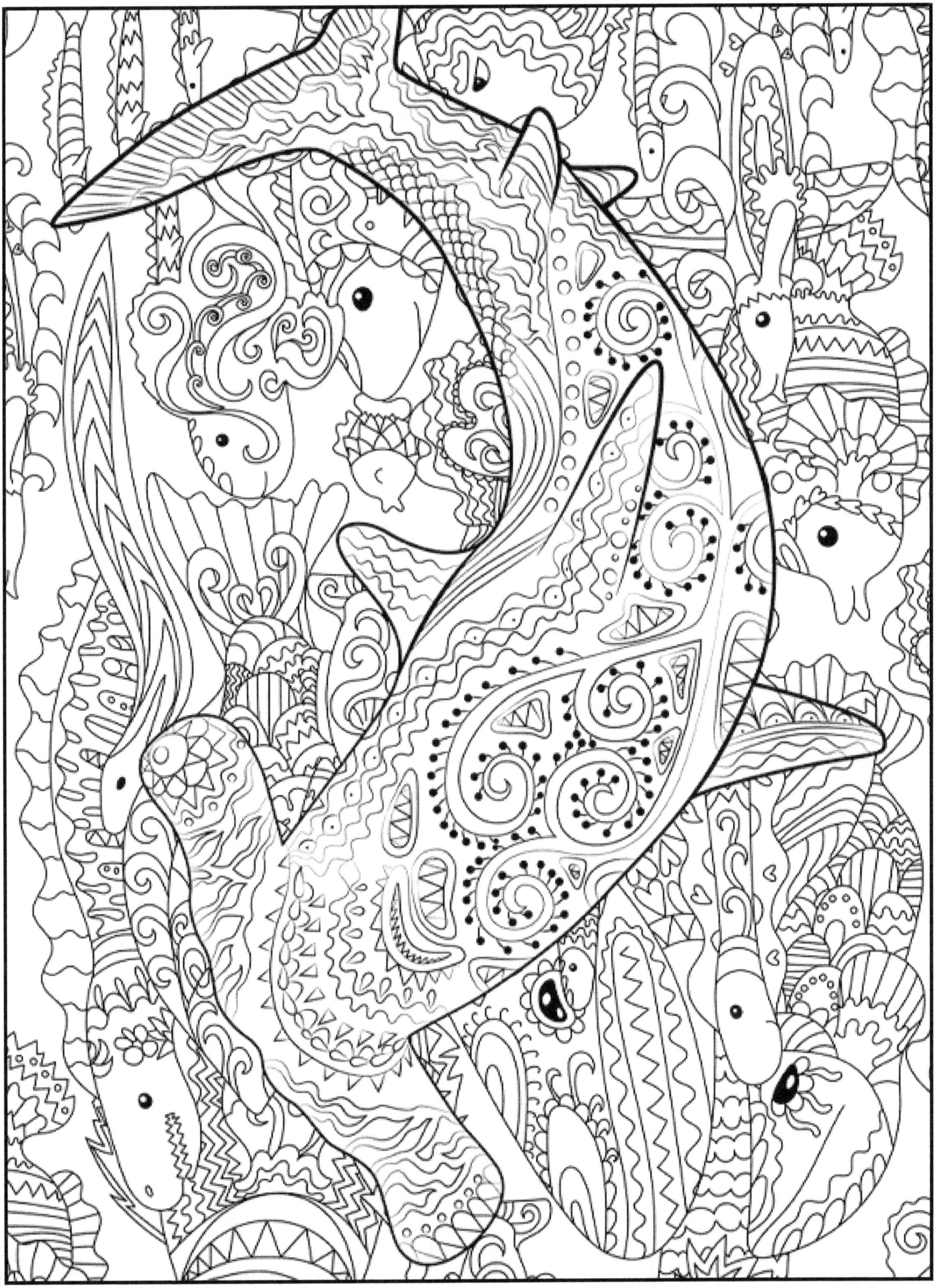

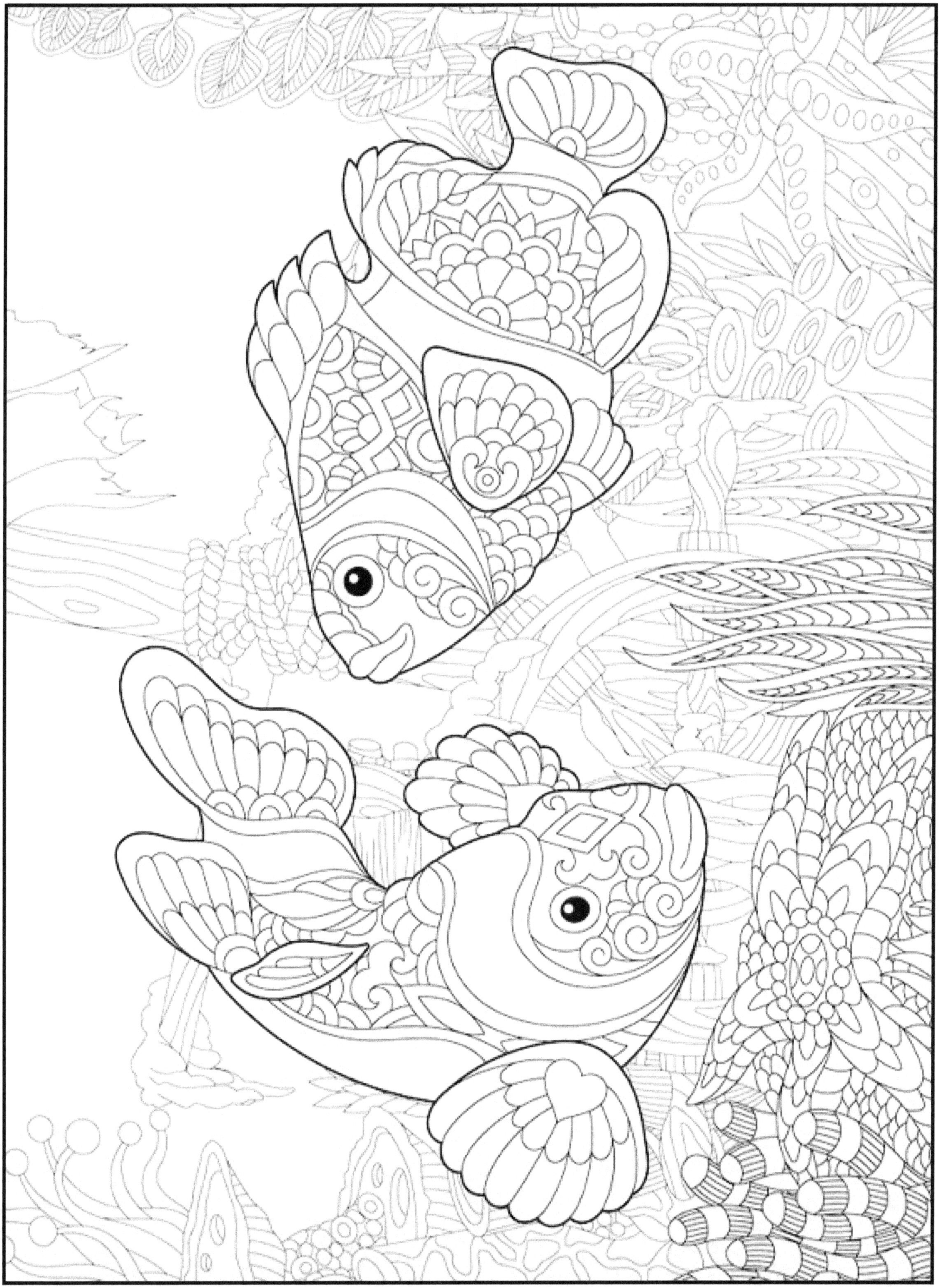

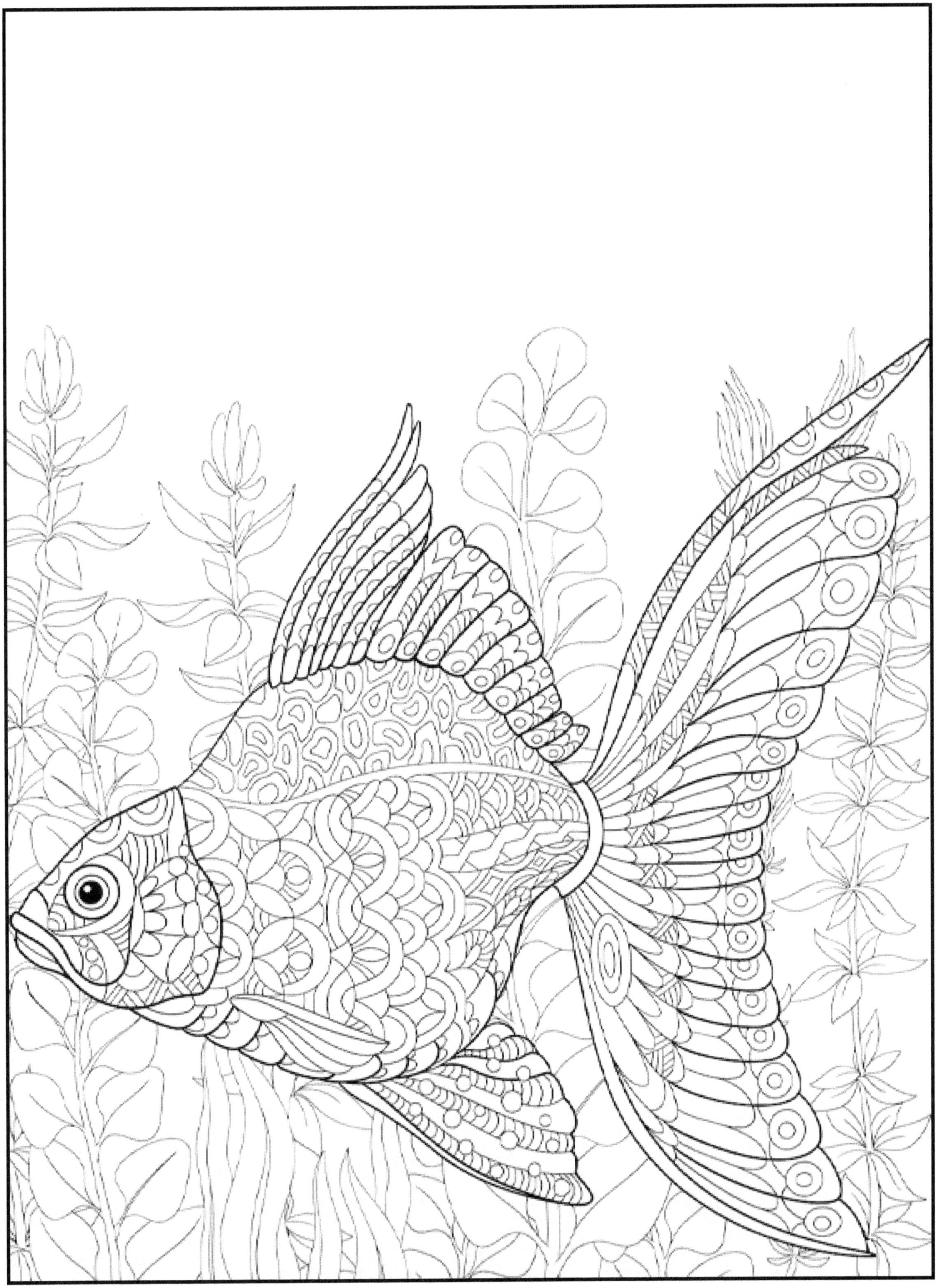

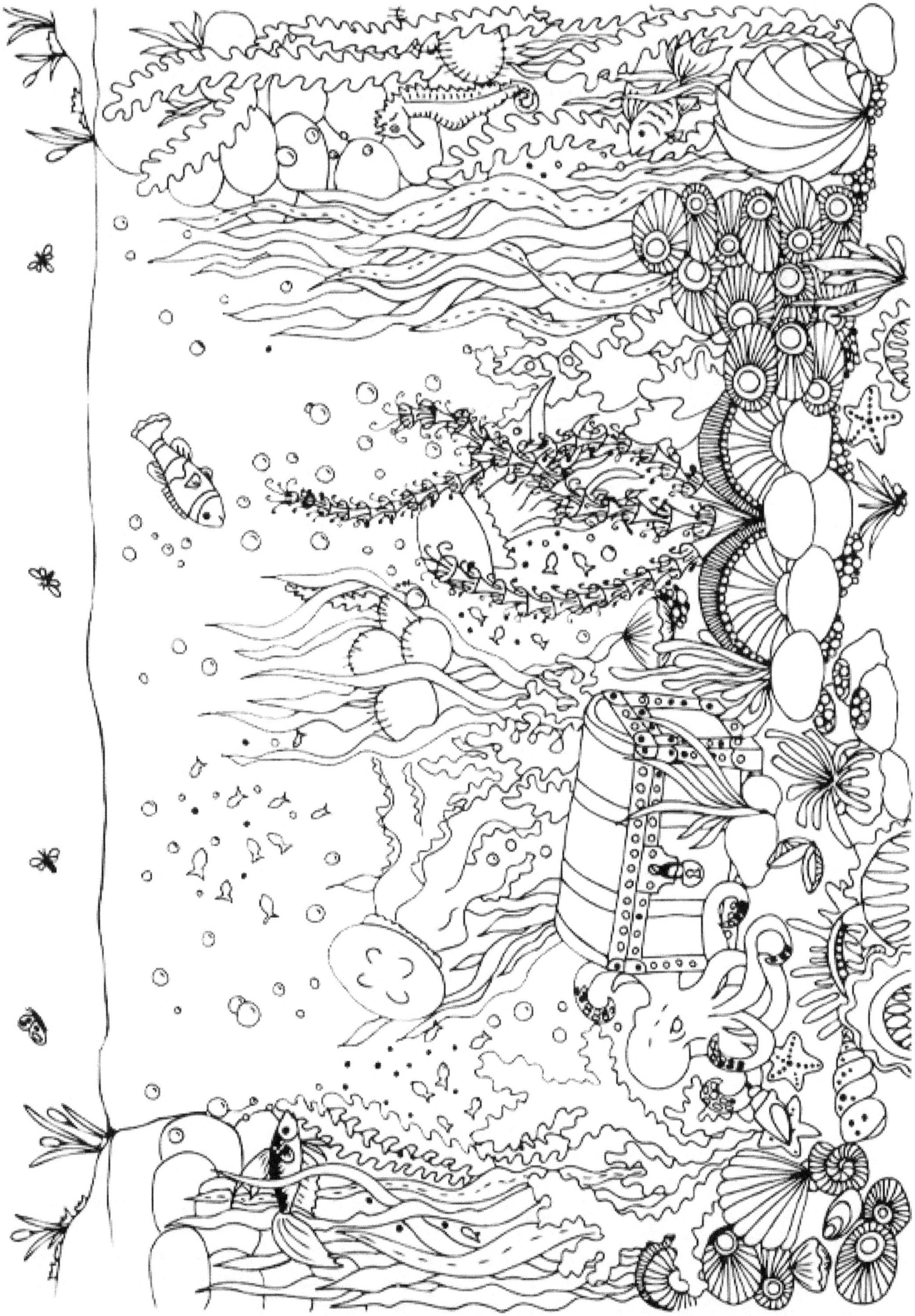

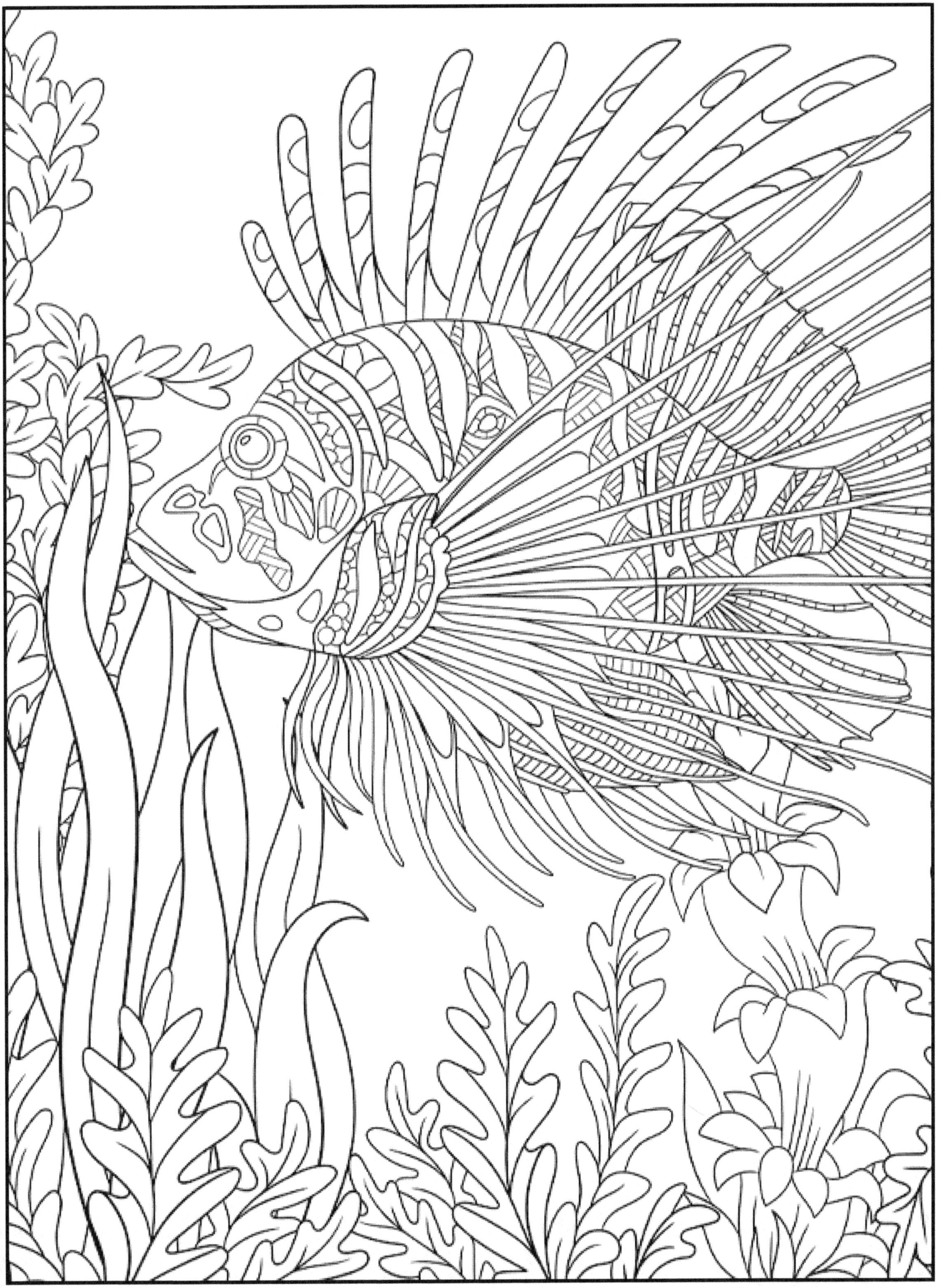

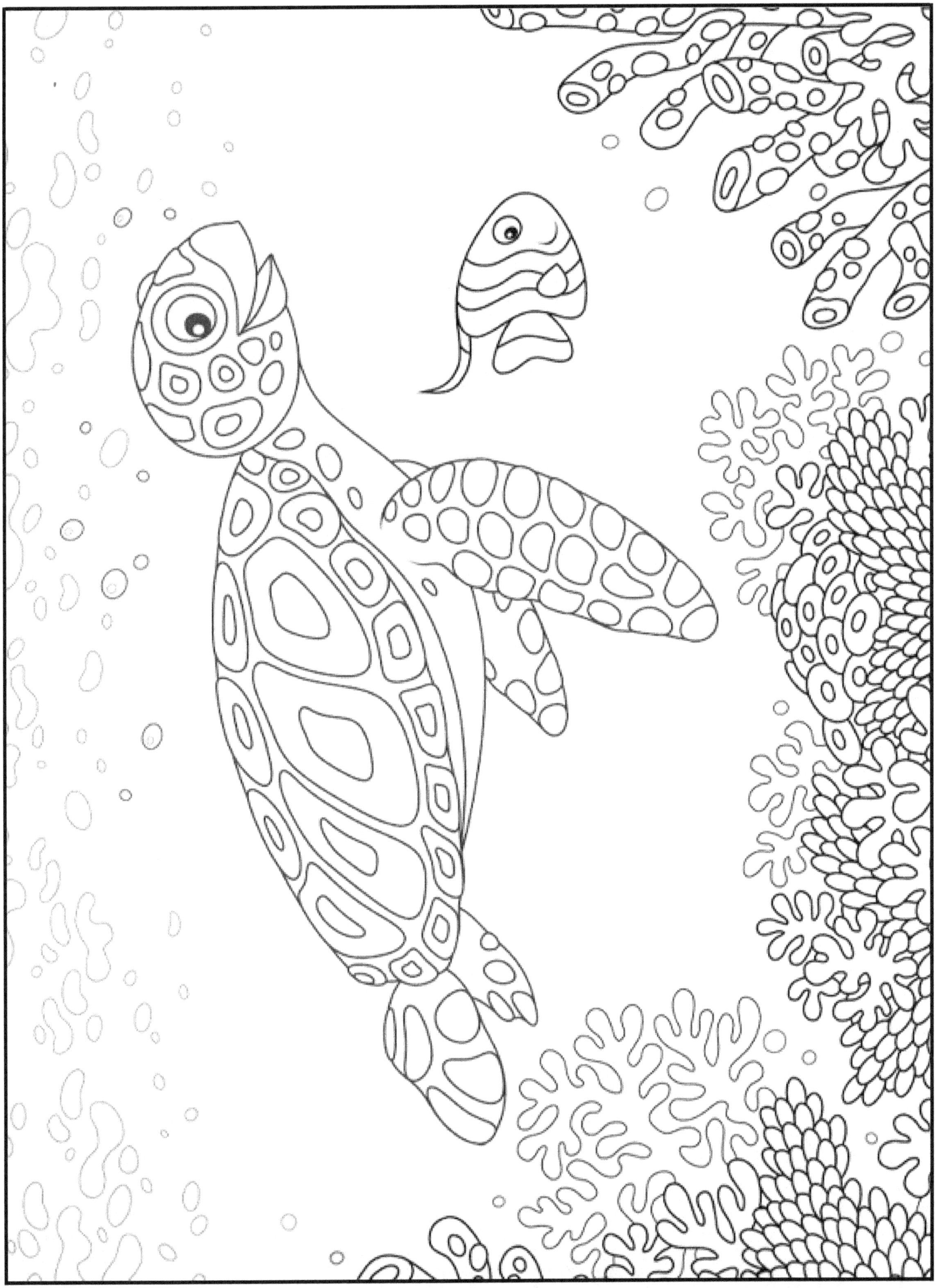

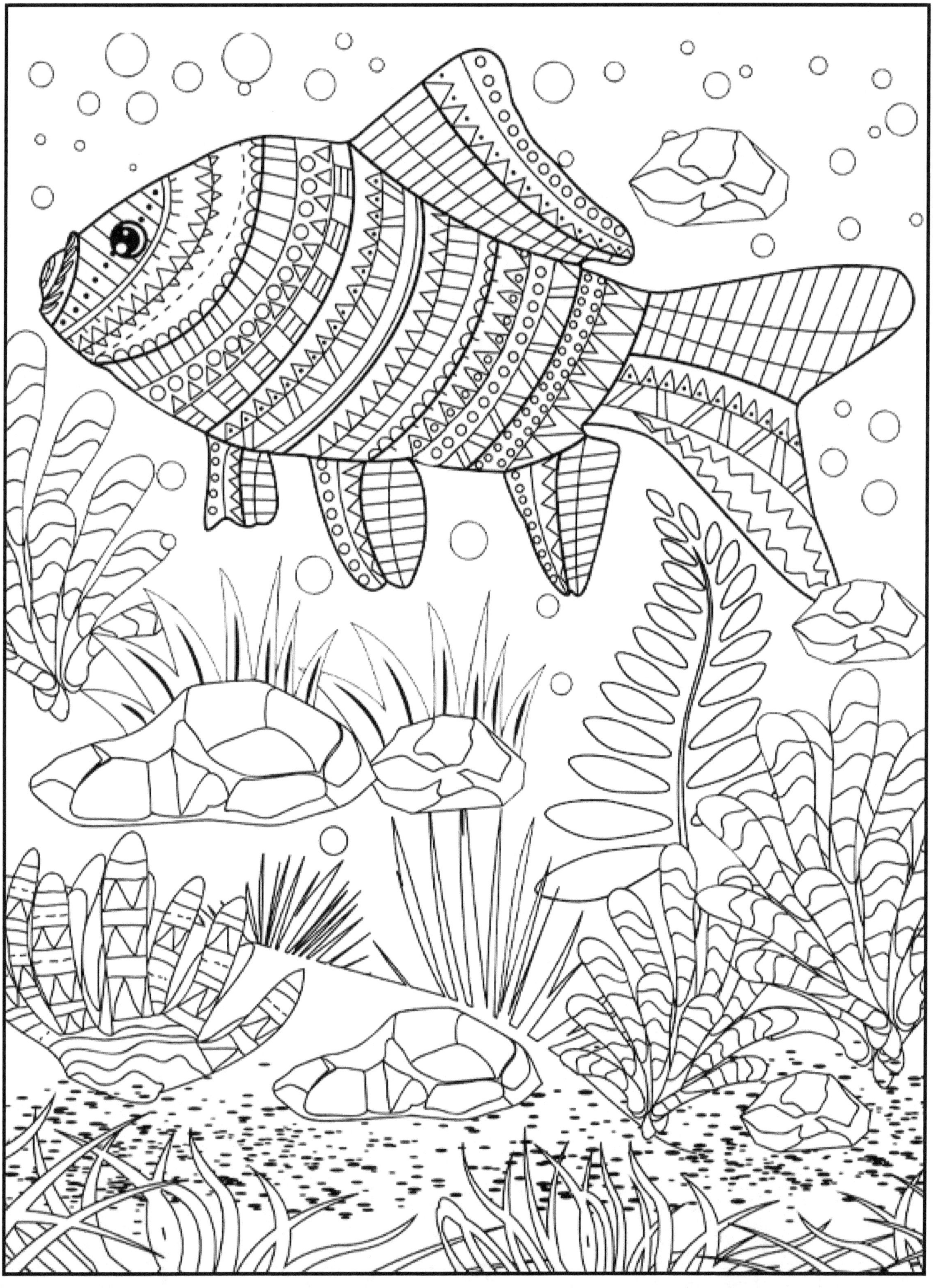

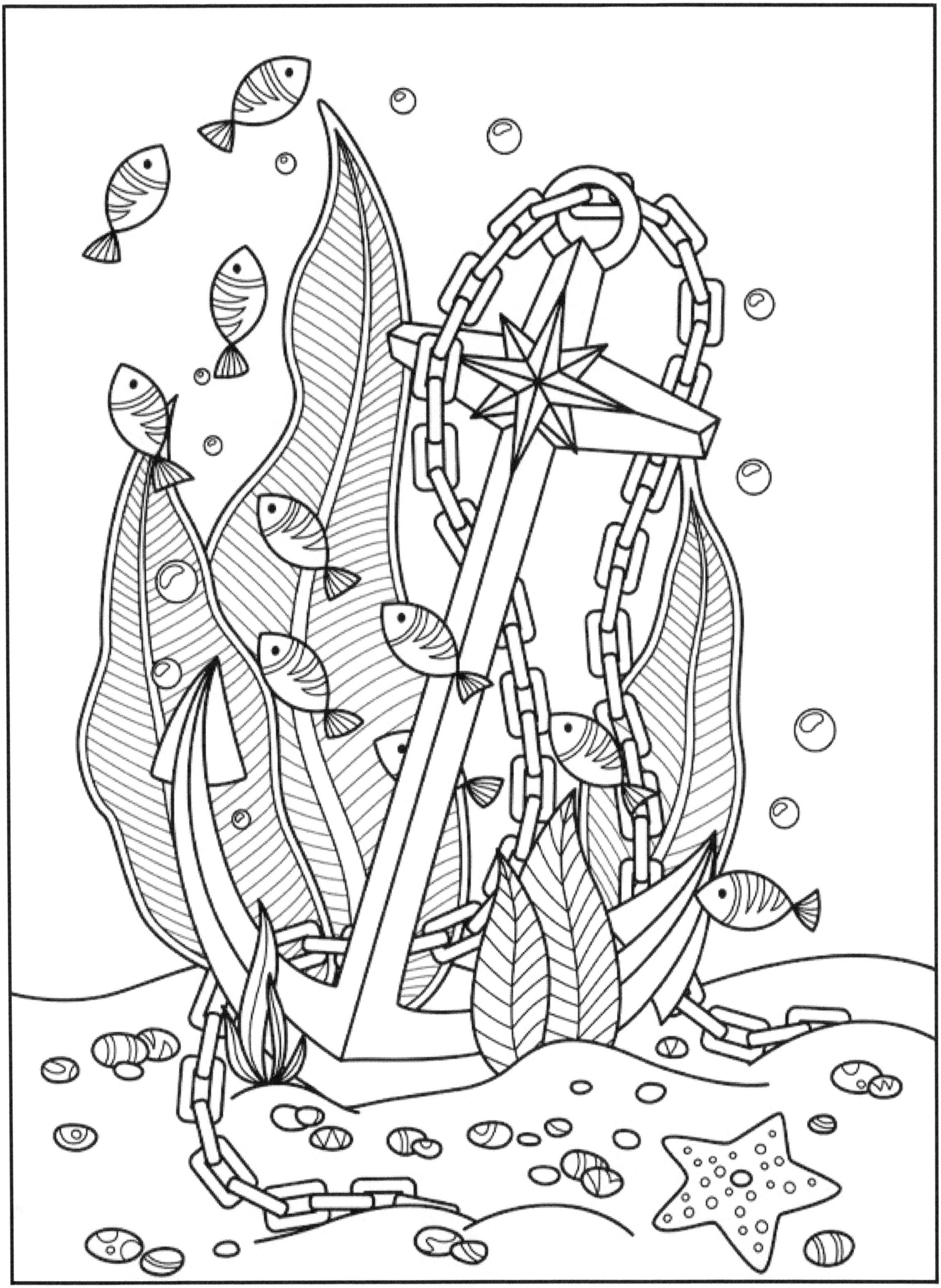

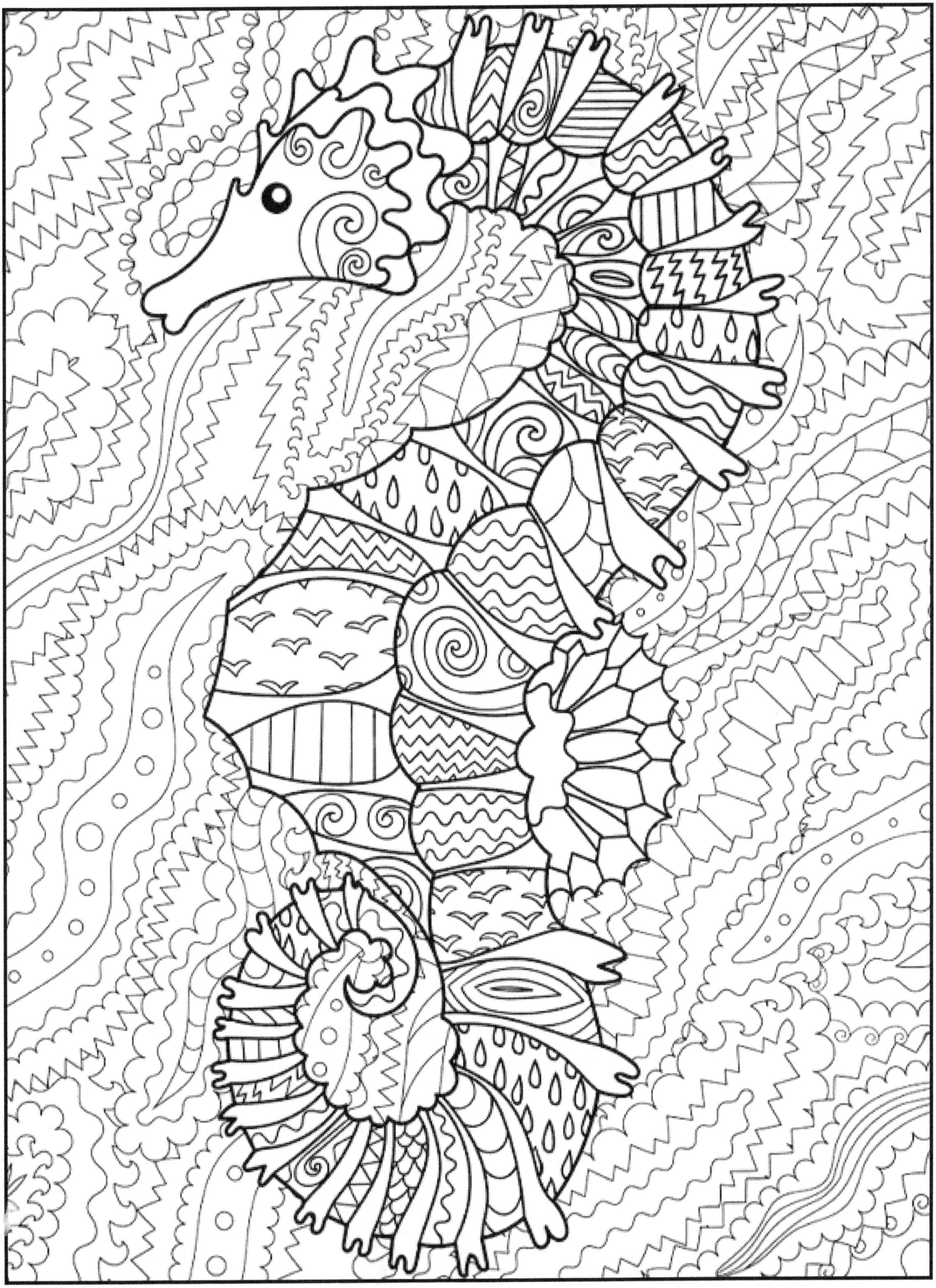

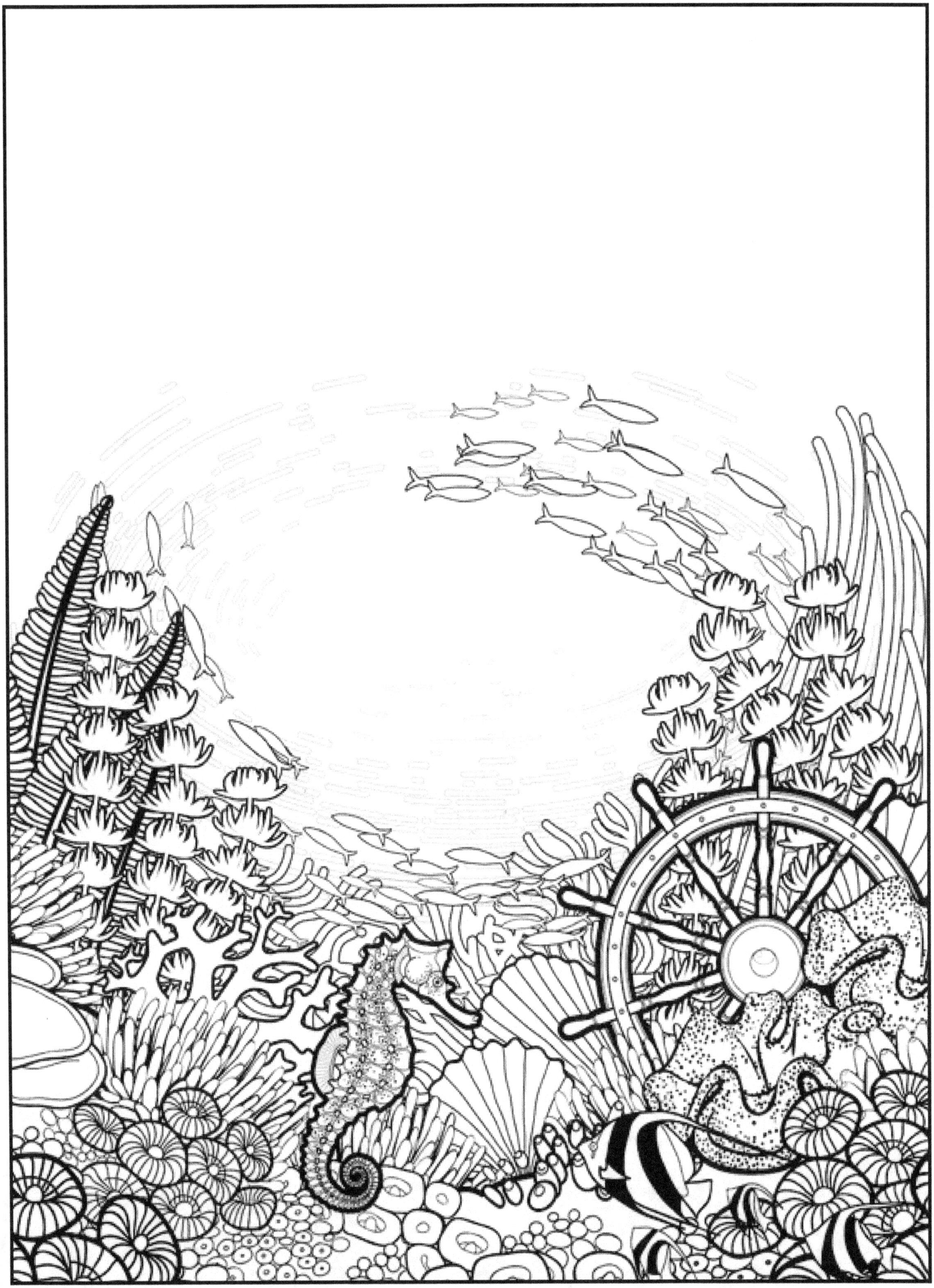

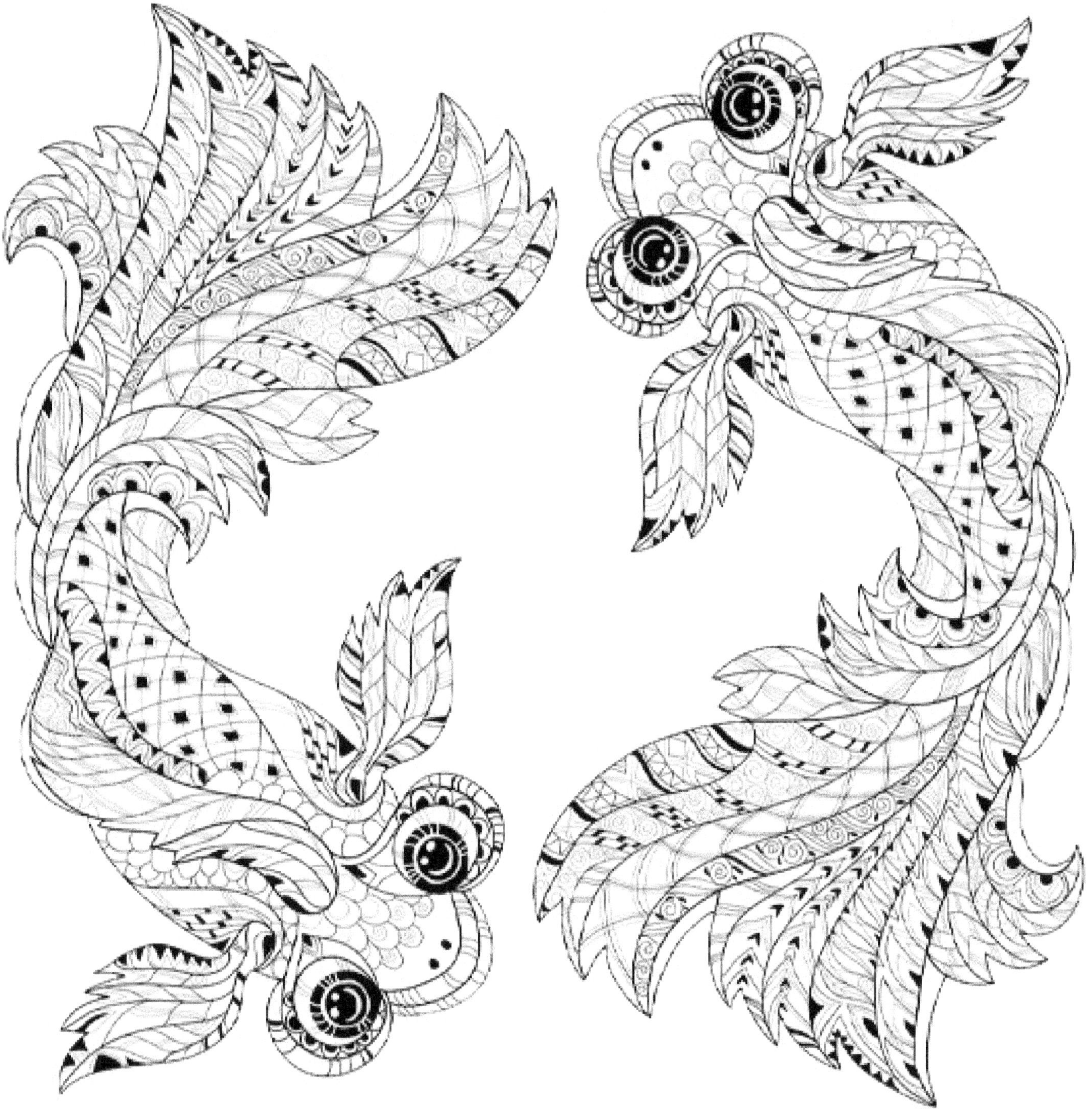

www.ingramcontent.com/pod-product-compliance
Lightning Source LLC
Chambersburg PA
CBHW080942170526
45158CB00008B/2342
*9781072925460*